The Beautiful Bridge of Death

*Accounts of Those Who Died,
or Nearly Died, in Falls from the
Golden Gate Bridge*

By Gene Donner

Donner

Contents

Notes and Observations..............................i
Chapter One: Who Are They?..........................1
Chapter Two: The Law of Concrete and Steel..........9
Chapter Three: The Flying Stuntmen.................22
Chapter Four: Those Who Jumped and Survived........34
Chapter Five: Those Who Tried and Failed...........50
Chapter Six: Fathers and Their Children............62
Chapter Seven: Couples.............................69
Chapter Eight: Those Who Left Notes................75
Chapter Nine: The Mysterious and Unusual...........81
Chapter Ten: The Grim Statistics...................95
Chapter Eleven: The Rescuers.......................99
Chapgter Twelve: The Battle of the Barriers.......113

"Who would want to commit suicide by jumping from the Golden Gate Bridge?"

>
--Joseph B. Strauss
>Chief Engineer
>Golden Gate Bridge

Donner

Some Notes and Observations...

As this was being written, residents of San Francisco and the Bay Area were wondering when the 1,000th suicide from the fabled Golden Gate Bridge would occur. This was moot since it already had...but not officially.

While doing research for this book, I discovered many discrepancies in the numbering of people who reportedly jumped to their deaths. Even in the early years there were inaccuracies in the news reports of these incidents (the fifth leaper was actually the sixth, the ninth was the 11th etc.) and the numbering became more confused as the list increased. The California Highway Patrol and Golden Gate Bridge District Authorities began keeping "official" records, but even these were not always accurately reported in the newspapers. When the Bridge District was formed the CHP became the official "police agent". After a suicide has been attempted or has taken place, it becomes a CHP concern. Officers even have authority to place those who attempt to commit suicide from the Bridge in mandatory confinement for 72 hours.

In order to be listed officially as a Golden Gate Bridge suicide, the victim must either be seen jumping by a "responsible person" or the body is recovered. It is difficult to state with any accuracy, but it is a certainty that several hundred--some say as many as 2,000--more people took their lives jumping from the Bridge than are listed in the "official" books. They either jumped at night or in a heavy pre-dawn fog when few were around to observe, and their

Donner

bodies were swept out to sea, although a statistical survey of a ten-year period from 1945 to 1954 revealed the greatest incidence of suicides took place during the daylight hours between 6 a.m. and 7 p.m. One reason for this is the Golden Gate Bridge, the only one in the Bay Area with a walkway, is only open to pedestrian traffic from sunup to sundown.

In March 1954, a California Highway Patrol spokesman reported 159 confirmed suicides and 63 "probables" in which clothing, notes, and unclaimed autos were found but "no positive evidence that a jump had actually taken place." The report was issued, he said, "because in the past many incidents had been referred to as suicides when there were no substantiating witnesses."

The total number of jumpers, therefore, has generally been assumed to be higher than what the CHP summary shows. It was also stated at the time of the above report, that there had been 80 attempts to commit suicide from the Bridge but these persons were rescued or dissuaded from committing the act. There have also been a number of "fake suicides" by people who want others to think they've taken their lives for reasons ranging from financial to love problems.

Years before the 1,000th leaper The San Francisco Chronicle (May 10, 1987) printed a tongue-in-cheek, "fictionalized" account of the event written by Michael Taylor. The story reported, in black humor style, that San Francisco officials decided to sell the 1,000th spot by sealed bid to raise money "for the families of small boat owners killed by the 84 jumpers who managed to miss the water beneath the bridge" (this was fiction, not fact).

Covered by all the major media, including network TV in helicopters, the "winner" was escorted to the center of the Bridge with much pomp and ceremony but then chickened out, to the consternation of the hot dog-chomping crowd who came to watch. The mob was so incensed they rushed the patrol car in which Mr. 1,000 and his police escort were making their retreat, and pitched it over the railing into the swirling waters below, so the story went.

While this was being written a radio station in San Francisco was forecasting that by the year 2,000 there would be 2,000 leapers. This did not sit well with officials who might have held "discussions" with the station.

The Golden Gate had a fascination for suicides long before the Bridge was built. Neill C. Wilson, in his *Here Is The Golden Gate*, (William Morrow & Co., 1962) wrote about a Capt. Norman Nelson, who was at the Golden Gate Lifeboat Station for 17 years in the early part of this century. He was credited with saving hundreds of lives, "intercepting about one hundred would-be suicides before they made the cold dive; dragged out another hundred more who got there ahead of him; and went, by boat or swimming, after still another hundred who succeeded in eluding rescue." He retired at 55 in 1928, having saved more lives than any other man in the U.S. Coast Guard.

My fascination with this subject began when I was a copy editor with the *San Francisco Examiner* watching the official number of leapers approach the 500 mark. This generated some editorial anxiety which resulted in a voluntary blackout of Bridge suicide stories until after the event. However, that didn't stop a surge of people trying to be number 500 as 14 attempts were recorded during this time.

"There were all kinds," said one officer, "including one fellow with 500 written on a piece of cardboard attached to his back. He said he was Jesus Christ. We got calls, 'I'm coming out tonight at five o'clock. I'm gonna be 500.' The pressure built up something fierce."

The "official" 500th leaper was a 26-year-old male blood technician at Franklin Hospital, who took the plunge on October 10, 1973. No one saw him jump but his body was found on the rocks below the north tower on the east side.

As I began making inquiries about the grim statistics, I experienced a certain reticence on the part of officials, no doubt because of the tenseness surrounding the pending 1,000th victim and renewed calls to erect suicide barriers.

After viewing a film at Fort Point made by Bethlehem Steel during the construction of the Bridge, I casually asked a Park Ranger if any suicides had landed on the structure, an ancient stone building built to guard the entrance to the Bay, situated just below the southern approach to the Bridge. It was also where Coast Guard rescue boats used to be stationed. The Ranger quickly glanced at me and scurried away saying she had something to do. I found out later that two jumpers had landed on the roof and were killed.

While taking photos of the suicide barrier in the Bridge district's "boneyard," I asked an official if I could talk to some Bridge workers and was told that they were under strict orders not to talk to anyone, especially the media, about suicides from the span.

During interviews with Coast Guard personnel I learned there had been a jumper just the day before one interview, but there was no report of it in the newspapers. Another officer said he was certain there was a "blackout" of suicide events until after the 1,000th statistic had been recorded.

This book makes no judgments about the people who took their lives or who attempted to do so. It is a straightforward account of those who fell or jumped off an edifice that has been eminently fascinating to millions of people

Donner

from its earliest conception through its amazing construction to the present where, in addition to being one of the foremost tourist attractions in the Western United States, is also one of the pre-eminent suicide venues in the world.

Donner

Chapter One:

Who Are They?

Statistical evidence indicated that the 1,000th "official" suicide off the Golden Gate Bridge would be a middle-aged male who would jump from the east side of the Bridge, as most do, facing San Francisco. However, that's purely hypothetical. It could just as well have been a lovesick teenager.

Male leapers have outnumbered women by a ratio of 3 to 1. The highest rate of suicide nationwide is among older white males, who make up 30 percent of all suicides but represent only 10 percent of the population. In 1992 the white population in San Francisco was 47 percent but accounted for 75 percent of the city's suicides. On average there has been one Bridge suicide every three weeks.

Ninety-five percent of the Bridge leapers are from the Bay Area with the rest coming from around the country and even from abroad. The youngest was a two-year-old boy who died (a few hours after he was rescued) when his father, clutching him to his chest, plunged in mid-span to the channel waters 260 feet below. The oldest was an 87-year-old man, who left a note blaming ill-health for his final decision. Several couples have jumped to their deaths, even a few stuntmen who unwittingly performed their final feat. There were three jumpers in a single day (see Chapter Eleven), and at least 19 known survivors--those who have miraculously lived to tell about the terrifying experience

(Chapter Four). One dog was reported to have jumped from the southern approach to the field below. The dog wandered onto the Bridge following some children on March 28, 1937, before it opened. When the children left, the dog, whose name was Pal, took the shortest way down, a 75-foot leap, suffering two broken front legs but was otherwise okay.

Early suicides from the Bridge were older, but through the years the median age has fallen to between 30-35 years, primarily, it is theorized, because younger people moved to The City from other parts of the country and apparently experienced difficulty fitting in. More Whites than Blacks jump from the Golden Gate Bridge, but the reverse is true of the Oakland Bay Bridge. The total number of leapers from the Bay Bridge is about one-third of those from the Golden Gate.

In recent years the majority of younger leapers--some say as much as 85 percent--have been HIV positive.

It is estimated that some 24,000 people commit suicide in the U.S. each year, about 65 a day (the worldwide total is about 1,000 a day according to World Health Organization statistics). Another 125,000 in the U.S. are treated after attempting to kill themselves. Suicide ranks 12th as the cause of death in America but is seventh in San Francisco which has one of the highest rates in the country, 17 per 100,000, according to a 1990 report, versus 12 per 100,000 nationally. Two decades earlier the rate for San Francisco had been as high as 30 per 100,000. Back then, The City ranked second, after Berlin, as the suicide capital of the world.

Despite its fatal lure the Bridge only accounts for 5 percent of The City's total number of suicides.

The reasons most often given for taking the final plunge are: a) troubled romance or family squabbles; b) emotional

disturbances; c) physical illness, and d) financial problems.
For every person who succeeds in leaping from the span six others who threaten to jump are saved by police, Bridge security, Bridge workers or Good Samaritans. In 1958 Patrolman Charles "Woody" Woodworth, then 35, was cited for saving a 27-year-old house painter from San Anselmo--his 80th rescue since working on the Bridge. Some leapers have almost taken their rescuers with them while others seemed glad to have been dissuaded from their grim goal. One woman became a "regular," making eight attempts to leap and showed up on the span three times in one month. When toll takers spotted her they immediately alerted authorities. She dropped out of print after that leaving a question mark as to her fate. Another woman tried to jump from both the Golden Gate and Bay Bridges but was thwarted in each case.

Among those who made the leap into eternity are celebrities, socialites, wealthy individuals, recently married, many more recently divorced or separated, mystery people, war veterans, young mothers, children of famous people, stuntmen, actors and actresses, models, housewives, bankers, dancers, contractors, teachers, ranchers and a generous cross-section of other professions and stations in life. Some made the front pages because of their status or their number, such as the 500th, while others barely merited a few paragraphs buried in the inside pages.

The Golden Gate Bridge officially opened May 27, 1937, promptly at 6 a.m. On that day the Bridge belonged to the pedestrians. Forever after it would be perpetually open to vehicular traffic.

(Except for five times -- the first being December 1, 1951 --when violent storms with gusts up to 70 mph screamed through the Gate causing the 220,000-ton, 740-foot steel

Donner

towers to sway several feet and the roadway to undulate violently. The second and third times were during equally robust storms in 1982 and 1983, when the Bridge had to be closed for several hours. The fourth occasion was in 1987 when pedestrians again took over the Bridge for the 50th anniversary celebration. They started marching in cadence but had to be stopped because the span began swaying. The fifth time was in the evening of May 9, 1995, when a man who was thought to be carrying a gun and threatening suicide, held police at bay, forcing them to close the Bridge to vehicular traffic for several hours. When the man made a threatening move with what looked like a handgun, police fired, hitting the man twice in the abdomen and once in the leg. (He was taken to a hospital where he was listed as critical).

On opening day the Bridge was jammed with pedestrians, and although passage was free, some slippery entrepreneurs charged a five-cent "toll" to unsuspecting out-of-towners.

When the Bridge was completed, Joseph B. Strauss, Chief Engineer and the one who bull-doggedly championed the feasibility of the project, was asked about people jumping off the magnificent edifice. His response was: "Who would want to commit suicide by jumping from the Golden Gate Bridge?" Early plans showed a railing much higher than the four-and-a-half foot railing that graces the Bridge today but was pared down ostensibly to allow an unobstructed view. An eight-foot "cyclone" fence was installed later along the southern approach to the Bridge up to Fort Point.

In late May 1937, there had already been one attempted jump from the Bridge but was "happily frustrated." The huge safety net used during construction was still in place, and since it stuck out ten feet on either side of the railing, it would have taken a determined and strong leaper to clear it.

The net was ultimately taken down because it swung too low to clear the tallest ships and gave less clearance than was promised the shipping industry before construction was begun.

An editorial in one paper on May 28 of that year stated (in language we find amusing today): "We don't know how much consideration or public spirit can be expected of the desperate ones who take their own lives, but we all hope they find other places and spare us the bad notoriety that has cursed the famous Arroyo Seco bridge at Pasadena and there is good reason to believe that they will if only because a jump from the bridge will by no means assure that speedy and painless death which most of the demented and discouraged seek."

In just a little over three months, on August 7, 1937, the first person made the historic leap from the fabled Bridge. He was Harold B. Wobber, a World War I veteran who reportedly was suffering from ill health. Before he jumped he removed his coat (as many of them did) and left a note saying simply, "This is where I get off."

Three weeks later State Highway patrolmen saved two people from taking the plunge. One was a 74-year-old woman who said she was "just tired of living" and wanted to jump because she had no money and couldn't get a pension. The other person, a sailor, had one leg over the railing before he was pulled back. He told police, "My life is worthless."

The 100th death leap came on June, 28, 1948; the 200th occurred in 1953; the 300th in 1966; 400th in 1970, and the 500th in 1973 (*see Chapter Ten*). There were 11 suicides in 1990, 18 the following year, 15 in 1992, and 21 in 1993. In 1994 there was an alarming and puzzling increase--30 death leaps with an additional 72 "reportable incidents." In one

48-hour period during that year two men jumped and one woman was escorted off the Bridge by the CHP. By May, 1995 the Bridge had "officially" logged more than 990 suicides.

The *Examiner*, in 1981, ran a story about some workers in a lumber shop in The City who, among their other sports betting pools, included a lottery on Bridge suicides with the official-sounding name of "The Golden Gate Leapers Association." Seven men would pick a day of the week and each put a dollar in the pot. The winner was the one who picked the day on which a person jumped from the span. In order for it to be "official," however, the story had to appear in one of The City's newspapers.

"It doesn't matter whether they live or die," said one, "it's strictly a pool, something funny, not morbid. We don't push anybody."

Posted on the shop's bulletin board were photos of horse racing and a picture of the Bridge with a chart listing previous winners and their "pots." If no one jumps, the pot keeps growing.

"You have to be of two minds," said a winner of one of the biggest pots, $121. "I wasn't pleased that someone leaped off the Bridge to their death, but I was pleased that I made a lot of money. This is like any other sporting event," said the big winner, who treated his buddies to a round of beers after work that day.

Many believe the Bridge has a mystique that lures people bent on taking their lives. There have been other such places, like Mt. Mihara in Japan where 619 people are said to have plunged into a smoldering volcano between 1933 and 1936. The suicides stopped when a fence was built and guards placed at the mouth of the volcano.

Another notable jumping off point is the 1,045-foot

Donner

Eiffel Tower in Paris. The Tower, built in 1889 by Gustav Eiffel, and the Golden Gate Bridge were running almost in a dead heat back in April 1968 with approximately 350 leapers each. From that date French authorities altered the Tower's grim listing. When the next Frenchman jumped to his death--reputedly because he lost his driver's license--he was not listed in ordinary sequence but one number lower and the number decreased from that point. The French stopped counting at 300 which is when they put up suicide barriers. The Eiffel Tower, incidentally, had another paint job in 1995--it's done every seven years or so--requiring a team of 25 painters working 14 months using 60 tons of "Eiffel Tower Brown" to cover the 18,000 metal pieces that make up the famous landmark.

The Empire State Building in New York City logged 16 suicides from 1931 to 1947 until a suicide barrier was erected.

The Arroyo Seco in Pasadena, California, accounted for 80 suicides before a barrier was erected in 1937, the year the Golden Gate Bridge was completed. Other bridges have had leapers but none so famous nor with so many as the Golden Gate, which is now considered the number one location for suicides in the Western World.

The first survivor of a jump from the Bridge was a 22-year-old woman. Her plunge was reported as 260 feet from mid-span, the higest point on the Bridge roadway. (The distance to the water at each tower is 220 feet, varying a few feet depending on the tide). Physicists computed her fall took just four seconds, with her body reaching a speed of 80 mph. When she hit the water it was with an impact equaling 15,000 pounds per square inch or the equivalent of jumping off a 20-story building. The tide had carried her 600 yards out to sea

Donner

in seven minutes before a rescue boat reached her. (*See Chapter Four on survivors*). She was the 35th person to leap from the span and the tenth woman.

Donner

Chapter Two:
The Law of Concrete and Steel

In 1846 John C. Fremont, a U.S. Army captain in the Topographical Engineers Corps, had his first glimpse of the entrance to San Francisco's seldom-used but breath-taking harbor. He named it the Golden Gate.

Two decades later Emperor Joshua Norton, one of San Francisco's celebrated and tolerated eccentrics, proclaimed that "a suspension bridge be constructed at Oakland Point to Yerba Buena, from thence to the mountain range of Saucillito (sic) and from thence to the Farallones," which lie some 30 miles off the coast. Most people at the time felt all three bridges were equally preposterous. But in the early part of the new century, the idea for a bridge kept surfacing. One persistent early "voice" was that of veteran newsman James H. Wilkins, a former mayor of San Rafael, who wrote about the possibility of a bridge over the Golden Gate with terminals at Fort Point and Lime Point.

By the "Roaring 20's" the concept of spanning the Golden Gate was being deliberated seriously, including discussions of overcoming countless hurdles, not the least of which was the "tremendous" cost, (Strauss' first estimate was $17 million -- nearly $40 million below another engineering firm estimate).

Construction of the Bridge was to be financed locally, with no federal or state funds, by issuing $35 million in bonds (the final cost) at a time when the country was in the midst of the greatest depression in history. (Replacement cost of the Bridge today has been estimated at $1.4 billion).

On January 5, 1933, after many years of frustrating wrangling, construction of the bridge across the Golden Gate finally began. For Strauss, who said: "It took two decades and two hundred million words to convince people the bridge was feasible," this project would be the crowning point of his career, one that had taken him around the world building more than 400 bridges.

At the time, three large suspension bridges existed in the country. The largest was New York's George Washington Bridge with a 3,500 foot clean span. Strauss' plans for the Golden Gate called for an unheard of 4,200-foot center span.

With a project this size there were bound to be setbacks-- and there were plenty--but as it moved forward month by month bridge workers knew something unusual was taking place, something that cheered yet terrified them. They were defying "the law of the concrete and steel," which is one life for each million dollars of construction.

As of October 1936, there had not been a single fatality, an incredible record, one that Strauss and his foremen diligently pursued by insisting on the strictest of safety measures. Everyone connected with the Bridge was proud of that record, especially because the elements seemed to combine to enforce the law of concrete and steel. Screeching winds gusting to 70 mph, slashing rain, murky fog or blinding sun glinting off the water was the Devil's own daily menu. The tiny flecks of human flesh crawled over planks and cables and steel more than 20 stories above a treacherous channel, where twice daily tides hurled 2,300,000 cubic feet of water per second through a mile-wide funnel at speeds between 4 to 8 miles mph.

One of the biggest reasons for this safety record was

Donner

the huge net that was slung under the Bridge that saved hapless workers who made a misstep or forgot to hook their safety straps.

Back in the early 1930's a company known as J.L. Stuart Manufacturing Company, (which later became the Stuart-Sauter Company) was called on to manufacture the huge safety net.

"The steel company considered putting up a net but never followed through with it," said Art Sauter, one of the former owners of the company. "Then our company was invited to work on it since we were involved in making tents requiring a lot of rigging.

"There was talk about trying to use a metal clamp which would be faster than weaving the net. The Larkin Specialty Co. did a lot of stamping of dyes and turned out small products, so we worked with them to develop this metal clamp. I believe it was patented although the clamp was never used after the bridge project.

"The net was a six-inch mesh, made of 3/8 inch manila rope supplied by the Tubbs Co. The clamps were of galvanized steel. A special loom was developed, 40 by 50 feet wide, to make the net.

"This was the largest net ever made," said Sauter. "It was built on the waterfront between the Ferry Building and Fisherman's Wharf.

"The steel company worked around the clock putting up the net. The crew strung a cable on each side of the bridge underneath and the net was lashed to the cables."

The enormous safety net cost $100,000 and went up in June 1936, as the girders for the roadbed began to extend from both sides of each tower, ultimately to connect to each anchorage and meet in the middle. This was designed to keep the load stress even on the two towers. Wags at the time wondered if the two sections forming the center span

Donner

would really meet at the center.

The net was destined to become a subject of mirth for some and a tragedy for others.

The first net "save" came on October 10, 1936, when an extremely strong gust knocked George B. Murray, 38, a carpenter, off the platform he was working on. His life was spared when he fell into the net 35 feet below suffering only minor injuries to his arms.

Eleven days later, on October 21, the papers heralded that "The mighty Golden Gate Bridge project claimed its first life." Kermit Moore, 23, a steelworker, was part of a crew working 1,400 feet out from the Marin shore. A traveling crane was laying steel for the decking. A pin pulled loose from the crane causing it to collapse, sending the boom of the crane hurtling into the channel below. The men working nearby included Moore, who was just about to get off a girder picked up by the crane. The men scrambled to get out of the way of the collapsing crane but Moore lost his race with death and was crushed between a support beam and the girder.

Miles Green, a fellow worker, was knocked off his perch by a whipping cable but was saved from the 220 foot plunge by falling into the protective net. He was not injured.

A little more than a month later, on December 4, riveters Jay Roberts, Paul Terry, and W. L. Wilson were slamming rivets into girders reaching their way toward mid-span. They were on a scaffolding 260 feet above the swirling green waters, and could see seagulls drifting lazily below them, passing in and out of the shadow of the gigantic structure. The roar and chatter of a hundred rivet guns exploding all over the bridge was so deafening the trio didn't hear the cracking of a plank on the scaffold as it splintered and broke beneath them.

In an instant Roberts and Terry dropped into nothingness

Donner

plunging toward the channel waters. But instead of certain death Roberts felt himself hit the net 35 feet below. A fraction of a second later Terry slammed into him, hitting him in the neck and back. Both men bounced on the mesh. They quickly glanced around for Wilson, then looked up to see him dragging himself by his elbows between two boards where he had found himself suspended after the center plank gave way.

During their sickening plunge neither Roberts nor Terry thought about the safety net. Roberts had the fleeting thought of "Well, it's all over," while Terry thought about his former wife. Wilson remembered shouting "Damn it," before scrambling to safety. The men were surprised later at all the fuss with reporters trying to interview them. Roberts told them his fall wasn't half the thrill of the time he fell several stories off a construction site in New York. At that time, he said, there wasn't any safety net and for the next eight months he spent a lot of time on his back in a hospital. The next day there was a new board in the scaffold, and Roberts, Terry and Wilson were back on the job.

Roberts and Terry were the seventh and eighth workers saved by the safety net. Those whose lives were spared started a club called "The Half-Way to Hell Club." Workers were falling into the net at the rate of one a month as the work pace intensified. Ultimately this exclusive club numbered 19 members. The frolicking daredevils who jumped into the net for fun or to retrieve fallen tools, helmets or debris were not eligible to join.

Steelworkers are a special breed of men who daily scamper around girders and scaffolding at heights that would make most of us giddy and weak in the knees. In 1936 they performed these wonders for the munificent sum of $1 an hour, or $8 a day. The saying was "8 for 8 or off the Gate." And since this was the middle of the depression, there were always men milling around the field office waiting for a chance to hire on for this high-wire act.

The wind was blowing hard with heavy gusts every so often on January 6, 1937. C. W. Brinkley had been working with his buddies 120 feet up, raising a false work tower for a derrick under the arch of the Bridge just above Fort Point. These gusts were making Brinkley nervous. He and fellow workers, J.J. Hollcraft and Robert Krieger, had just taken away the wind brace when Brinkley saw it coming -- a "Taku" wind. He knew that Taku winds were sudden, sweeping blasts that come out of the Taku inlet in Alaska.

"Let's get the hell out of here," he yelled to his pals but realized it was too late. The tower swung away and back and out again, prompting Brinkley to shout above the roar, "Here we go lads, it looks like a long buggy ride." As the tower shuddered and started keeling over, Brinkley shouted, "Good-bye and good luck, boys."

Brinkley was shot over the Fort onto the courtyard. Dazed, he started crawling to a nearby wall. A carpenter came up and asked him how he got down so fast.

"I didn't take an elevator," he replied.

Brinkley and Krieger were both lucky, and after being treated for bruises, they were back on the job the next day. Hollcraft was not as fortunate and suffered a broken back.

By February 1937 most of the steelwork on the Bridge had been finished and men were racing to complete the cement roadway. Evan C. Lambert, 27, a foreman on a cement crew, arrived at work on February 17, 15 minutes early as usual. He looked over his tools and greeted his friend, Fred Dummatzen, 24, and other members of the crew as they began showing up. A trace of darkness still lingered as they prepared to go

Donner

aloft.

    Lambert thought of going for a quick cup of coffee but time ran out and he had to scoot. The morning was calm and unusually warm for February. He and Dummatzen made plans to go out for a few beers on the weekend as they traveled to their work site midway in the span, directly over the channel where the water is 350 feet deep.

    Lambert and his crew were working on a five-ton traveling stripper, a platform suspended beneath the bridge from clamps attached to the bridge girders and moved by a hand winch. On the 20-foot by 10-foot platform a scaffold was erected enabling the men to work beneath the span removing wooden forms used to lay the concrete paving for the Bridge roadway. This device was something new, and today would be the first day it was used. The men were a little leery of it.

    It was even warmer in the partially sheltered area where they worked, and the crew could smell the familiar whiffs of tobacco smoke coming from Tom Casey's pipe. The men joshed the red-headed, 28-year-old about his constant "companion," which was forever clenched between his teeth.

    As the crew started work they chatted about what they had brought for lunch even though it was not even 9 a.m. Thirty-five feet below them was the vaunted $100,000 safety net that had allowed the Golden Gate Bridge project to cheat the "law of concrete and steel." Two workers were in the net gathering up debris from the preceding day.

    Lambert was informed earlier that there would be a safety inspection team coming sometime that morning to check the traveling stripper. They wanted to make sure all the parts were solid and in good working order. At times, Lambert felt all this emphasis on safety was a nuisance, but he couldn't deny that it had paid off in lives saved.

Donner

    Lambert, Dummatzen, Casey, Terrence Halliman, Casey's 29-year-old buddy, and seven others were on top the stripper, pulling away the wooden concrete forms when suddenly Lambert felt a shudder. He looked up at the clamps and then at Dummatzen. In that instant one end of the stripper pitched downward as something gave way. "Jump," Lambert shouted to his crew as he leaped from the stripper and plummeted to the net. As he was trying to get his balance he heard a sound like thunder, looked up and saw the five-ton stripper and scaffolding hurtling toward the net. Luckily he was out of harm's way but he knew some of his men had probably been hit by the metal monster or the scaffolding.

    Though this was all happening in an instant Lambert saw the net sag as the five-ton stripper hit, almost as though he were watching a slow motion film. There was a loud crack as the net snapped in the middle, then 2,100 feet of it began ripping loose from its cabled outrigging along the sides toward the San Francisco pier. The entire net fell into the channel carrying its human cargo with it. Some said later the popping sounds of the net ripping lose from the two cables could be heard in Marin County.

    Men were screaming all around him as the net tore like tissue paper and plunged toward the water. Some were hanging on or were trapped in the netting. Some were probably already dead, crushed by the stripper and platform. Lambert clung to the net with all his strength. As he was falling a piece of timber gashed the side of his head knocking him unconscious, but when he hit the icy water he came to instantly.

    Tom Casey, who was at the rear of the scaffold, felt the first shudder of the stripper and was instantly alert. When the stripper wrenched loose from the front, he was propelled up and managed to grab one of the clamps from which the stripper was suspended. He hung on with all he had, listening to the snapping of the net and the terrible screams of the men below. When the stipper hit and the net gave way, he felt the entire Bridge shudder. Other workers watching the horrible scene hung on for dear life while the Bridge towers rocked back and forth as though in an earthquake.

Except for the cut on his head from the flying timber, Lambert was not injured. A strong swimmer, he quickly assessed the situation, and paddled to get clear of the net and wreckage that were quickly sinking and being pulled out to sea. As he drifted with the outgoing tide he spotted three pairs of feet sticking out of the water, trapped in the net. He tried to swim to the spot but couldn't make it against the 5 mph current. As he watched, horrified, pair after pair sank below the surface, as though sucked down by some sea monster. He thought he saw three other men clinging to the wooden wreckage, but they were gone when he looked for them again.

He closed his eyes for a second to clear the salt water and when he opened them, he spotted one man floating about ten feet away. As he swam toward him a terrible expression came over the man's face, and Lambert knew he was dead. The body sank before his eyes. Then he saw Fred Dummatzen. He swam as fast as he could toward him but it seemed to take hours. Dummatzen was alive but a dead weight in the water. Lambert grabbed at a piece of timber floating nearby, hauled Dummatzen onto it and stayed with him praying to be rescued quickly so Fred would be all right.

As they drifted through the Gate toward the open sea Lambert's body felt like a block of ice. He heard the long blast of the field office horn summoning everyone off the Bridge, a tradition in construction work when a death occurs. Blood was running into his eyes from the cut. He felt that

Donner

all around him were the bodies of his buddies and he couldn't do anything to help them.

For 30 minutes Lambert floated hanging onto Dummatzen hoping help would come before it was too late. He thought of his blood spotting the water and wondered if sharks were around.

They were about a mile from the Bridge now. Lambert was exhausted and just about to give up when he heard the throbbing of an engine and saw through blurred eyes what looked like a boat coming toward him. It was a fishing boat returning to its berth at Fisherman's Wharf, skippered by Mario Mendella. Mendella maneuvered his boat alongside and pulled up Dummatzen, aided by Lambert with what seemed like his last ounce of strength. Then Lambert was hauled aboard. When they examined Dummatzen they discovered he was dead.

Casey was unaware of the tragic toll of lives below. He was too busy trying to save his own. He dangled 260 feet above the water for seven minutes--it seemed an eternity-- before someone heard his shouts for help. Workers hauled him up to safety with a rope. His feet once again on solid surface, he grinned and said, "That was a close shaver."

This is Casey's own account written in a letter to his mother:

"Dear Mother: I better be telling you what happened because you'll be hearing about it anyhow. Me and some of the boys were working on the scaffolding underneath the bridge. We were about 300 feet up (sic). When the scaffold gave, about 12 of the boys went down but your son Tom didn't. The luck of the Caseys, mother, it was. And me 300 feet hanging on like a monkey. So I holler's up at the boys, 'throw me down a rope' I says. The first one that came down was thin and greasy. There was no knots in it. I figure I might as

Donner

well let go rather than shinny up that. So I hollered up 'nothin' doin'. Send me down another,' so they did. A Casey never lets go, huh mother? But your son couldn't have hung there much longer. Just as simple as that. And take it from me it felt good to be standing on my feet again. And I never let go of my pipe either. I had her in my mouth all the time. And that's all I know, mother. It's nothing to worry about because it's all over now. Your son, Tom Casey."

Albert Tedd, a painter, told his own version of how Casey cheated death.

"There was a red-haired carpenter working on that scaffold who sure likes his pipe. He's Tom Casey, and when the scaffold crashed he had his pipe between his teeth. We yelled for him to stick and William Foster, an inspector, and I lowered a rope to him.

"We had a loop in the end and got it between his legs. Then we told him to let go and ride on up. He did, and we pulled him up, with that darned pipe still stuck in his face, and nothing between him and the Bay but the rope.

"When we got him up on the bridge deck he stood there, white and shaky a moment, then started to say something. When he opened his mouth the pipe fell out, but I'm a liar if he didn't catch it before it hit the roadbed.

"Casey stuck it back in his mouth and walked off, with only 'Boy, that was a close shaver.'"

Casey, who was forever after to be known as "the thirteenth man," 12 having gone down in the net, lost his friend, Terrance Halliman.

"My buddy lies there at the bottom of the Bay," he said. "I can't forget that."

Capt. Douglas Burrowes of the tugboat, Tango, towing a barge to Fort Baker, witnessed the tragedy from the pilot

Donner

house.

"The net sheared away from the bridge and lashed toward the water like a big cleaver wielded by a giant hand," he said. "It ripped back toward the tower, fell splashing into the water and was borne away by the strong tide then running. I didn't see any bodies fall clear."

Earl Bradshaw, one of the first bridge workers to join the rescue effort said, "I was painting on the bridge near the scaffold that collapsed and carried away the safety net below it. It made a noise like a million firecrackers. I looked to that direction and saw the scaffold and net falling, carrying the men with them. It paralyzed me--I couldn't move for a minute. I could hear the yells of the fellows who were caught for a few seconds, then their shouts were drowned by the cannnonade of sound.

"I climbed to the bridge deck and ran for the San Francisco tower. That end of the net was still secure and for a minute I thought about using it to get down to the pier. But while I looked at it, the net jerked loose from the tower and plunged down to the water."

Scores of boats raced to the scene hoping to find survivors. They searched for more than five hours in vain. Attempts to retrieve the net by grappling hooks also failed. Later, however parts of the net were retrieved with some bodies still wrapped in its deadly web.

As the men trudged off the worksite, some were cursing, some were crying, many were just silent. Jack Bishop, a painter working above the terrifying scene, said "I've seen men die before. I've heard their death cries. I've been in the worst storms on sea and on land. I've been in deafening thunder. The terrific noise of this catastrophe was a combination of all of them...only worse."

Donner

Investigators determined the cause of the accident was a defective aluminum caster supporting the stripping platform and a lack of sufficient bolts. On March 17, Strauss stated that faulty design of the caster units was officially to blame for the stunning tragedy.

"Parts of the net were retrieved," recalled Art Sauter, but a replacement net was made. The salvaged net was brought back to the shop and eventually disposed of.

"Some criticized the net after the accident," he said. "But it was never meant to withstand the impact of five tons of steel and equipment. It gave the workers a sense of security and was credited with speeding up construction and reducing costs.

"I have no idea what became of the net. As for the patented metal parts, we kept some around for a while, and then they, too, became part of history," said Sauter.

The two men who were in the net picking up debris were rescued. Ten died and 19 were injured in the early morning tragedy that in a few moments shattered a 44-month safety record and once again proved "the law of concrete and steel."

The toll of bridge workers didn't end with this. After the severe December storm of 1951, it was decided the Bridge needed some shoring up. It was during this time that another collapsing scaffold resulted in the deaths of two workers. Two painters also lost their lives, one in 1967 when he fell from a scaffold and his safety line broke, and another in 1972 who also fell from a scaffold but landed on the Marin shoreline.

Donner

Chapter Three:

The Flying Stuntmen

On Septemeber 21, 1939, just two years after the Bridge opened, Charley Boyd Delps and his wife/assistant, Lillian, walked into Central Emergency Hospital in San Francisco and announced "I jumped off the Golden Gate Bridge a few minutes ago." Astonished medical personnel gaped. "That's right," echoed the wife.

"Look at my clothes," the 32-year-old stuntman said. The nurses looked at his unmistakably wet clothes.

"I took pictures," said the wife, "but I'm afraid I was so nervous I missed getting him."

When the roll of film was developed it showed Delps in the water, but there was nothing showing how he got there.

Delps said a friend was stationed in a boat below the Bridge and "towed him ashore." In an attempt to prove that he jumped, the stuntman pointed to a cut on his right leg he said he got crawling over rocks while coming ashore.

Doctors examined Delps and said he had a slight concussion but were unable to say how or when it occurred. They treated his leg and told him he could go home.

Delps said he had been planning the leap for years, even as the Bridge was being constructed. He had contacted another stunt diver, Kay Woods, who jumped in March 1937 from the Oakland Bay Bridge. The 186-foot plunge left Woods with a broken back and unable to walk. Delps said he landed feet first and that the wind didn't bother him. He wasn't

surprised people were skeptical about his jump and said he
would do it again if he could get a sponsor.

"I'd like to get back to stunting in Hollywood," he told
reporters, "that's the reason I jumped today. I'm a stuntman,
and I'm looking for publicity."

Golden Gate Bridge authorities and toll plaza police
said they had no report of anyone leaping from the Bridge.
The Coast Guard, stationed at Fort Point, also had a negative
report. It is not known whether Delps got his Hollywood job
as a stuntman.

- - - - - -

Frank Cushing's Thrill Circus wasn't doing all that well
financially and he was hoping to get a GI loan to infuse more
life into it, "not only for myself but for other fellows," he
said. A decorated Navy hero, the 44-year-old had just
received a medal a week earlier for rescuing a wounded
shipmate from a flaming destroyer off Okinawa during the last
stages of World War II. Cushing performed a high-diving act
in his circus so his plan of garnering publicity and
increasing the prospects of getting a loan was a natural one-
-do a really big dive--from the Golden Gate Bridge.

That was in April 1947. Although times were getting
better, many GI's were still finding it difficult being
assimilated into the labor force.

As of this date, 77 people reportedly jumped from the
Bridge. Only one lived to tell about it. Years earlier, on
Oct. 7, 1940, there was a report that a self-styled champion
stunt diver named "Speed" Needham, made the 260-foot leap
from mid-span and lived. But he never came forward to claim
the title nor did the Coast Guard find a body. A California

Donner

Highway Patrolman did find a bundle of clothes on the bridge near the San Francisco side, and a six-page note that said in part: "I'm going to conquer the Golden Gate's tides below and claim a new record. They arrested me twice but I went ahead and made a record dive of 120 feet off the bridge in Cleveland. I will build a stairway to the stars and dive off the top of the tower if I get the movie rights." Bridge authorities doubted the note and passed it off as an attempted publicity stunt.

Cushing claimed his longest jump thus far had been a 165-foot plunge from the Manhattan bridge 12 years earlier. He "took a beating on that one," he said, because he had not been prepared. He and John "Ace" Sutherland, a friend and member of the circus troupe, had discussed the idea of Cushing's jumping off the Bridge as a trial run. Later he would do the Oakland Bay Bridge as a publicity stunt that would draw attention to their need for a loan.

Cushing, his wife, Marjorie, and Sutherland gathered in Cushing's small hotel room in the early hours of April 14 to make the final preparations for the event. They went over the details for the umpteenth time as Cushing donned three pairs of trousers and a special sponge-rubber padding over his legs and torso. In a large carrying bag he packed a crash helmet and a Mae West life jacket. In a separate bundle was a one-man collapsible life raft with a 30-foot length of rope attached. At 3:30 a.m. the three of them, together with the Cushing's two small children, Marjorie, 4, and Frank Jr., 2, got into Cushing's circus truck and headed for the Bridge with Sutherland driving.

At that time in the morning there was little traffic so they drove to the center of the span where Cushing and his wife got out. Sutherland drove the truck, with the sleeping

Donner

children, to the north end of the Bridge and waited. Cushing attached the collapsible life raft to himself with the rope, donned his crash helmet and climbed over the railing facing the roadway. He gave a quick smile and small wave to his wife and then pushed off.

He didn't make any somersaults as he plummeted but stood upright the entire way down, throwing the life raft out in front of him. He hit the water at a speed of approximately 80 mph, and blacked out momentarily. He was on the surface when he came to and immediately started pulling the raft to him. He yanked the plunger to inflate the raft and then clambered aboard. The tide carried him seaward although he tried paddling to stay close to the Bridge. He spent more than two hours in the raft and drifted about three miles west of the span before he was spotted by Skipper Manual Nato, who was returning from a night of crab fishing. His boat, appropriately enough, was named "SOS."

Cushing's wife watched the descent as best she could in the pre-dawn dark but did not see the life raft open. She panicked and raced to the Toll Booth shouting frantically that her husband had just "jumped from the Bridge to get a GI loan." An immediate search was launched but before the Coast Guard could get to the scene, Cushing had already been rescued.

Nato, the skipper of the "SOS", listened to Cushing's fantastic story and, being a simple man, did not know what to believe. What he knew for sure was that only one person lived after jumping from the Bridge and she was badly injured. His wife read the story to him from the newspaper. He also knew this fellow on his boat, if what he said was true, might need medical attention so he brought him to the Fort Point rescue

Donner

station.

Cushing was taken to Park Emergency hospital where he told a doctor that he felt all right except for some back pain and being a little hungry. The examining physician said Cushing showed no signs of injury or submersion, but conceded the effects of submersion could have dissipated during the two or so hours from the time he hit the water and was brought to the hospital. The ambulance crew, used to transporting the mangled bodies of leapers, remained somewhat skeptical.

Cushing countered, saying, "Don't forget, I'm a professional stuntman, I wasn't trying to commit suicide."

Reporters asked if he still planned to jump off the Bay Bridge.

"I don't think so," he replied, "unless there was some money involved."

(When my ex-wife, a TV reporter on Guam, read this chapter she said she knew Cushing's widow and children, who were then living on Guam. The son, Frank Jr., apparently took after his father doing daredevil stunts, and is well known on the island).

- - - - -

It was going to be the jump of his life and it proved all too true. Thirty-eight-year-old Alfred "Dusty" Rhodes had been a Hollywood stuntman and daredevil in barnstorming tours for a number of years. He had appeared in the film, "Duel in the Sun," in which he jumped from a cliff, and was frequently called to do stunts for action films. He made substantial sums of money filling in for the stars during hazardous sequences but apparently very little remained. His career was in decline and needed a dramatic boost. He thought of the Golden Gate Bridge.

Donner

    Rhodes spent three months planning the stunt, according to his estranged wife, Lorraine, boasting that "It would be the greatest stunt of my life." Rhodes' Los Angeles agent said Dusty tried to get permission from Bridge authorities to do the stunt a year earlier but was turned down. Although Mrs. Rhodes and Dusty had been separated for several months, she was there to watch the jump. She and the two children, Oalla, 9, and Rocky, 5, were living with her mother in Port Chicago at the time.

    The night before the "big leap" Rhodes invited his wife, Walter McRoberts, an Army buddy, and a photographer named Jose Guzman to his hotel room in San Francisco for final instructions. He and Guzman agreed to a 50-50 split of the proceeds from the sale of a motion picture film Guzman was going to make. During the course of the evening Rhodes turned to McRoberts, and said, "There's one thing I want you to promise, that you'll take care of my wife and kids in case I don't make it. If I make it, I'll have publicity and be on my way."

    Very early on the morning of February 6, 1948, the stocky, 170-pounder began getting ready. Like Cushing, (perhaps he had read reports of that successful leap), he put on heavy underwear, several pairs of trousers and sweat shirts, and around his hips a pair of pads used by football players. He put on all this paraphernalia very dexterously even though two fingers were missing from each hand--the results of previous stunt mishaps. In addition to a crash helmet, an inflatable rubber life suit--the kind used by merchant marines--and a Mae West life jacket, he was also going to use three small parachutes to brake his fall. His earlier plan included strapping 50-pound weights to each foot to prevent him from spinning in the air, but at the last moment he decided not to.

Guzman, meanwhile, was getting all this on film. It was nearly time to leave. Rhodes glanced at the bottle of whiskey on the small table in the room and poured half a glass. He raised the glass in a silent toast to those in the room and gulped it down. Guzman recorded him kissing his wife and his two children, then walking out to a car arm and arm with his wife. The children stayed behind.

It was mid-morning and traffic was beginning to thin after the commute. The group drove to mid-span where Rhodes, his wife, and Guzman got out while McRoberts drove to the Marin side. Lorraine said she "wanted to give Dusty moral support," and agreed to accompany him even though she tried many times to talk him out of the leap.

Guzman kept filming Dusty as he made his way along the Bridge's east sidewalk looking twice his normal size with all the equipment he had on and carrying the folded parachutes. People in passing autos thought perhaps a movie was being made. They were right, to a degree.

When Dusty climbed over the railing and perched on the catwalk on the other side, two Bridge maintenance workers, Arthur Olsen and Charles Crandall, observed him and ran over. Olsen reached over the railing grabbed one strap of Dusty's life jacket and asked him what he was doing. "I'm all right. I'm prepared for this," said Dusty. In the next instant he twisted away and plunged downward leaving the broken strap dangling in Olsen's hand as he watched Dusty's descent.

Mrs. Rhodes and Guzman thought the parachutes would allow him to glide down. The parachutes opened but were worthless as Dusty dropped like a rock. Mrs. Rhodes was torn between looking and not looking. She couldn't help

Donner

herself and saw him "hit the water like a bullet." She saw his head bob out of the water, and it looked like he was waving or trying to swim.

Guzman was filming all the while getting Dusty as he hit the water, went under, came back to the surface and then began drifting out to sea. They didn't see the life raft open. The Bridge workers immediately notified the California Highway Patrol and Coast Guard, who recovered Dusty's body. Rescuers said he might have survived if he had popped the inflation cord on his Mae West.

Mrs. Rhodes was dazed by the tragedy and didn't remember leaving the Bridge but somehow she made her way back to her mother's home in Port Chicago. When police arrived at the jump site they tried to take Guzman into custody but he said he was a photographer who "just happened along." His photo of Dusty leaping from the Bridge was used on the front page of the *San Francisco Examiner* the next day.

Guzman said he hadn't sold the rights to the movie film, although he had offers from numerous news agencies, because "it was the last thing Dusty did and it was a failure." The film was shown two weeks later, however, at a coroner's inquest, during which Mrs. Rhodes buried her face in her hands several times as she watched. The jury's verdict was that Dusty died by accidental drowning.

A young District Attorney by the name of Edmund G. Brown, who later became governor, told reporters he was looking up the law to see if The City could prosecute those who "aid and abet stuntmen in their jumps."

- - - - - -

People are oftimes inspired by the actions of others and perhaps it was Dusty's unsuccessful parachute attempt from the Bridge that lead Bob Niles, 22, to seriously consider the

Donner

stunt.

An ex-Army paratrooper instructor with more than 85 jumps and now an aerial stuntman based in Oakland, Niles intended to make a big splash by becoming the first to parachute from the Bridge and live. He was working with an Oakland film maker and his stunt was to be part of a film called "Thrill Seekers." He was also planning a barnstorming tour of daredevil jumps throughout the state in the summer.

Set for March 26, 1949, the stunt wasn't exactly a state secret. Niles had alerted a dozen friends who were to be in boats poised under the Bridge to retrieve him. The media somehow got word of the pending "first" and newspaper and newsreel photographers had assembled in mid-span. One San Francisco newspaper wanted to get an exclusive but Niles wasn't interested.

He was driven to the Bridge by a pilot friend who had flown him on many of his previous jumps. The car passed through the toll plaza and proceeded to just beyond mid-span, where Niles jumped from the car and hurried toward the railing, where a gaggle of newsmen and photographers were waiting. Niles' wife, Betty, the Oakland film maker and several news photographers were on one of the dozen boats bobbing in the water below, while a helicopter froze itself in position about 100 feet from the railing where Niles intended to jump. He never made it.

A California Highway Patrolman stepped out from the crowd as Niles started to climb the railing and escorted him to a waiting patrol car. He was brought to the Toll Plaza for questioning and then turned over to San Francisco police on charges of committing a public nuisance and disturbing the peace. He was given a ten-day suspended sentence. Niles vowed he would try again next month and keep returning until he

Donner

made the jump.
    Niles made good on his promise. This time, he kept the plan to himself. On April 15, 1949, at about 1 p.m., he was driven to the bridge by a friend. The car stopped about 100 yards toward the Marin side of center-span. Niles jumped from the car, ran to the railing and climbed over the side. He eased himself down onto the ledge just below and then let go. In an instant the white plume of his parachute was visible as he drifted on a westerly wind that blew him about 100 feet east of the Bridge. He hit the water gently, the chute spreading out on the water in front of him. Although he had friends on a boat stationed below the Bridge, a suspicious Coast Guard crew reached Niles seconds after he hit the water and brought him to the Fort Point station. As could be expected, a number of drivers stopped when they saw the stuntman going over the side. The Bridge was tied up for a while as several near accidents occurred.
    Although he got into trouble for that stunt it didn't prevent him from making the news yet again less then a month later when he made a 505-foot jump from the tower nearest Yerba Buena Island on the San Francisco side of the Bay Bridge. A strong wind carried him about 50 yards from the tower where a cabin cruiser, piloted by a friend, picked him up moments after he landed. This time he was given a sentence of 30 days in the county jail.

- - - -

    A Hollywood film crew known as Motion Pictures International was preparing to shoot a jump scene from the Bridge July 14, 1970, for a film titled "P.S. I Love You." The film stared Peter Kastner, playing an advertising executive, who was supervising a simulated leap from the

Bridge. Stuntman Frank Orsatti was to pretend he was going over the railing to jump, then the camera would pick him up flying through the air, but the actual jump was from the top of a crane moored off Fort Point. Although the crew had arrived very early to set up the "shoot," it had been postponed because of the heavy fog pouring through the Gate that morning. A San Francisco radio station had noted that fact during a morning show and announced the stunt was rescheduled for 12:15 p.m.

All "official bases" had been covered with every jurisdiction alerted to the film company's plans for the day. Every precaution had been taken so that gawking drivers wouldn't snarl the Bridge traffic with a nightmarish pileup.

It is possible that a 27-year-old Berkeley man had heard the radio station's announcement about the stunt and decided to watch. He headed toward the Bridge, arriving in plenty of time to view the interesting proceedings.

The camera crew had earlier shot the scene near the south tower of the Bridge and had now set up for Orsatti's leap from the crane. A Bridge security sergeant had been watching some of the action on the television cameras set up on the lowest crossbeams of the two towers to monitor traffic and also, more recently, to watch for anyone acting "suspiciously." The sergeant could not see the Berkeley man, however, because he was behind the south tower watching the stuntman climb the 100-foot crane.

At 12:15 p.m. the signal was given for Orsatti to make his jump and the cameras started rolling. The jump was successful, and the stuntman, who was paid $5,000 for the part, was retrieved uninjured. While scores of spectators were mesmerized with this Hollywood make-believe scene, the Berkeley man quietly climbed over the railing at 12:17 p.m.

Donner

to make his final scene in this world, falling 220 feet and landing in the moat around the base of the south tower. The sergeant, who was notified of the event by an observer, and other Bridge officials were stunned. The Coast Guard recovered the man's body, the 383rd official leaper from the Bridge.

Chapter Four:

Those Who Jumped and Survived

On the last day of January 1995, at the beginning of the morning rush hour from Marin County, people saw a 42-year-old woman perched on the outside east ledge of the south tower. She was clinging to the railing and looking down when two California Highway Patrolmen pulled over and gingerly approached. They tried to talk to her, but she didn't respond, just kept looking down. As the officers got nearer she "just let go," they reported.

From her position at the south tower, she fell 220 feet and landed in the moat created by the fender at the base of the tower. The fender serves to prevent off-course ships from crashing into the tower and to ward off the pounding waves and heavy current. The officers radioed a hasty report and descended to the moat area on the slow-moving tower elevator. The water level inside the moat is 15 feet from the top of the barrier, so it was difficult for the officers to reach the woman who was "making swimming motions."

They extended a wooden pole to her outstretched hands and tried pulling her in, but she was too weak and one arm was injured. The officers threw a net into the water, positioned the woman over the top and pulled her up. She was given emergency medical treatment aboard a Coast Guard cutter then transferred by ambulance to Marin General hospital.

Donner

This woman was the latest (as of this writing) to join a very exclusive group of "Survivors," those who jumped from the Golden Gate Bridge and lived. Their number varies because the figure gets confused by reports that include both the Golden Gate and Bay bridges, but one thing is certain, they are rare. Of those listed as "survivors," several died minutes or hours later and one ten days after the fall. The survivors recounted in this chapter do not include the two stuntmen described in Chapter Three.

- - - -

The charter member of the "Survivors Club" was a 22-year-old woman who plunged from the Bridge on September 3, 1941. She was the 35th recorded leaper and the tenth woman to jump from the Bridge.

It was one of those perfect days in San Francisco. An almost cobalt blue sky was unmarred by clouds. It was warm but, as usual, a bit windy. Julia (not her real name), had the afternoon off from her State job and decided to walk to the Bridge. She had been very tired and irritable for the past several weeks and felt guilty because her mother was taking the brunt of her foul mood. She and her soldier boyfriend, stationed in Albuquerque, had been corresponding regularly, and although they considered themselves "engaged" she felt uneasy about the longevity of their relationship.

Julia sauntered to near mid-span and paused to gaze at the sparkling City, sun glinting off its white buildings and making some of the streets look as though they were paved in silver. Peter Bamm and a fellow painter were on a scaffold about a third of the way up the south tower putting on a new coat of "Golden Gate (international) orange." Bamm nudged his buddy and nodded to where Julia was standing at the railing as both continued to watch her. Many bridgeworkers develop a sixth sense about potential suicides--something about their actions that give them away. As the two watched, debating whether to call the CHP, the girl climbed over the railing, perched on the other side briefly and then dropped.

Falling 240 feet, she slammed into the water in just four seconds (although it seemed like an eternity to her), and was traveling at approximately 80 miles per hour, according to physicists. With an impact of 15,000 pounds per square inch, it was like hitting cement. The painters heard her screams after she hit the water and saw her floating far below. Bamm got to the nearest phone and notified police. A Coast Guard speed boat and a Navy lifeboat raced to the scene arriving within seven minutes. In that time Julia had drifted 600 yards seaward before she was pulled unconscious aboard the Coast Guard boat.

From a hospital bed she talked about her "irresistible impulse" to jump, saying she "looked at the water and all of a sudden the water came swirling up at me and then I jumped. I don't remember much about going down except that I felt numb. I was conscious all the time." She denied intending to commit suicide or that she had written any note before her leap.

Attending physicians were amazed she was alive. Her arms had "snapped like matchsticks," she sustained a compression fracture of her back, severe bruises on her legs and internal injuries, but medical experts said she wouldn't be paralyzed. When she was later visited by her soldier "fiance," she was able to walk into his arms.

Asked if she felt lucky to be alive, she replied, "Oh yes. I'd never do it again and I certainly wouldn't advise anyone else to try it."

- - - -

Although well-intentioned advice, it was to be ignored

Donner

by the many hundreds who followed her path over the railing.

    - - - -

The second person known to have survived the plunge was an unidentified man whom police described as in his middle 50's. This occurred on February 25, 1946 and was recorded as the 59th person to leap off the Bridge. A patrolman saw the man leap and rushed to the south tower to take the elevator to water level where he saw the man floating. The patrolman shouted over the wind and waves asking his name. The man replied, "That's for you to find out." He died before the Coast Guard arrived.

    - - - -

On December 12, 1961, a 20-year-old Oakland man, who was "afraid of cops," jumped and lived, but died 10 days later.

    - - - -

A 16-year-old boy from Livermore was observed climbing the railing in mid-span at 4:15 p.m., on January 11, 1965. Bridge officials were alerted and one patrol car and one tow truck were dispatched to the scene. (The reason for the tow truck is that leapers have been found to be curious about the arrival of a tow truck, and the distraction has often brought them back from the railing. A police car produces too dramatic an effect with sometimes fatal results).

A lieutenant at the Toll Plaza scanned the east railing with binoculars but couldn't see anything at first, but as the men in the tow truck stopped, he glimpsed the boy jumping, feet first with hands held above his head. The men ran to the railing and saw the boy come to the surface within minutes. At that very moment, the 12,000-ton freighter, the Korean Bear of Pacific Far East Lines, was bearing down directly toward the lad, who was now swimming. One of the tow truck men set off flares signaling the ship to turn to starboard. A quick acting helmsman saw the signal, and the big vessel slowly began to turn, missing the lad by ten feet.

A crew member aboard the Coast Guard cutter speeding to the scene spotted the husky lad "treading water, his right arm waving in the air as if he was trying to get our attention. His tan sweater was up around him like a life preserver." As the cutter came alongside the boy struggling in the choppy water, the crew asked if he were hurt or had any broken bones. The boy responded in the negative and the crew put a litter into the water and hauled him aboard.

"He mumbled a couple of things and was conscious all the time, his eyes were wide open. I guess he was pretty scared," reported one crewman.

At 4:30 p.m. the cutter arrived at Fort Point where a waiting ambulance took the lad to Letterman Army Hospital in the Presidio. At the hospital he lost consciousness for nearly an hour and remained unidentified because all police found on him was a dollar bill and 17 cents in change. When he regained consciousness he told doctors his name so parents could be notified and was then placed in the intensive care recovery unit.

Doctors said the boy's youthful vigor was a factor in his survival. Although he was "in good condition, completely alert and talking coherently," they kept him in the hospital for several days for observation. He had suffered a broken collar bone and three broken ribs. The boy told doctors he was walking on the Bridge "and the next thing I knew I was in the water." He was the fourth known span survivor.

Just two weeks earlier a 36-year-old Oakland mother jumped 230 feet from the Bay Bridge and was rescued alive by the Coast Guard.

- - - -

The fifth person to survive a Golden Gate Bridge leap

Donner

was another teen lad who had, strangely, met and talked with the fourth survivor, according to his mother. The Oakland boy went to mass and confession on the morning of April 30, 1967, and then spent time walking The City before taking a bus to the Bridge. He joined the scores of other pedestrians in mid-afternoon, watching boats criss-cross the Bay as brisk breezes ballooned their white sails. He paused at the south tower and carefully climbed the railing. Most strollers' gazes were fixed on the scene below, and before anyone could intervene, the teen was hurtling 260 feet to the water.

The Coast Guard was immediately summoned and rescued the lad as he started swimming toward shore. He was taken to Letterman hospital and was reported to be fully conscious and in good condition, but was held for a few days in the intensive care unit. The lad's mother told authorities he had been under a psychiatrist's care. As of this date there were 317 known suicides from the span.

- - - -

"It was like eternity flying through the air like an angel. I felt as if it would last forever," said the sixth survivor, a 26-year-old self-styled poet who earned his living as a portrait artist at Fisherman's Wharf. His "blissful" experience occurred on November 3, 1969.

"Getting my foot over the rail was the hardest thing," said the artist, who admitted an earlier attempt to jump from the span. "Surviving was easy. It doesn't seem so high when you're falling. The water was nice when I hit it. It was cool, calm and restful, almost friendly. When I splashed I wasn't conscious until I was swimming, then it was fun. Until then my eyes were closed. When I opened them I wasn't surprised to be alive. Even though I tried to do away with myself because of disappointment over my work and the disappearance of my poodle, when I opened my eyes there was no need to worry anymore," he said.

Within minutes of hitting the water he was picked up by the skipper of a fishing boat who said, "Look, we caught a wet duck."

Recalling the view from the Bridge, the leaper commented, "No matter how depressed I felt, the City looked so lovely and the Bridge, it had such an eternal splendor about it. It's such a beautiful way to go."

Recovering from a ruptured spleen and a fractured right leg, the injured artist/poet said he was going to concentrate on "enjoying life for a while" and dedicated a poem to the previous survivors.

- - - -

Early in 1971 there was a much publicized account of the "body that got up and walked" toward his rescuer. A 21-year-old Stanford University student jumped near the north tower and landed on the jagged rocks and sand of Lime Point. When the officer sent to investigate arrived at the spot where the man jumped, he looked down and saw him sprawled on the ground and assumed the victim had died from the 180-foot fall. As he was about to leave to retrieve the body, he saw a hand move. He sped to the area below, and as he arrived "the body gets up and walks toward me in a daze," the officer recounted.

The student was the seventh known survivor escaping with only broken collar bones and contusions. Officers speculated his ski jacket might have filled with air as he fell, slowing his descent.

- - - -

The 435th known leaper became the eighth survivor on November 11, 1971. On that morning, the 36-year-old IRS worker got up as usual in his Pacifica apartment where he lived with his wife and two children, a daughter, 11, and a son, 4. The family had been packing for a move to Fresno so there were boxes stacked throughout the rooms.

When he woke up that morning the tax expert felt depressed and that he was "no good." "I had time on my hands, started getting more depressed and made a resolution I would kill myself right away," he said, stating that he had been depressed all his life and was constantly under a doctor's care.

While his wife was busy getting their daughter ready for school and making breakfast, he quietly slipped out of the apartment, got into his Ford Falcon and drove to the Bridge. He parked on the San Francisco side near the Round House restaurant. It was just past 10 a.m. and the weather was foggy, raining, and cold as he walked to the south tower and climbed the railing.

"I was hanging on, waiting, asking 'do I have the guts?' Some man came running out of the fog yelling at me. I got mad, cursed him and let go."

He said he was not immediately sorry he jumped. "I had my arms outstretched like Jonathon Seagull. On the way down I felt, 'Gee, this is a long way down. I kept trying to go outside but the wind blew me toward the concrete moat at the base of the tower. I thought, no, I want to die a noble death."

His feet hit the water first and his back slammed against the concrete fender of the moat. He never lost consciousness until he hit the water but was "out" for a few seconds, before he started swimming and yelling for help. He found a notch in the concrete with his finger and held on until he was rescued.

Donner

"At first I didn't see anything but a bunch of tires and garbage, then I saw him treading water and more or less hanging on," said a Coast Guard crewmember who climbed up on the concrete wall of the moat. "I threw him a life jacket and told him to put it on but he mumbled something about 'I can't, my chest,'" said the Coast Guardsman.

Rescuers reported that the leaper was conscious but gave no explanation for jumping. At the hospital he underwent a spleenectomy and treatment for serious chest and liver damage as well as a punctured lung and back contusions.

Two years later, on March 27, 1973, he was interviewed by the San Francisco *Examiner* and said, "It doesn't bother me looking," pointing to the railing by the south tower where he jumped, "but I do have a certain amount of apprehension about walking out there."

Asked why he jumped, he replied, "I'm not really sure. I'm still asking myself. I think I may have been possessed by demons, I was crazy. I'm in the process of getting sane again, but I still hear voices."

A Catholic who drifted away from the church but now called himself a Christian, he said he survived because "there was some higher person helping me."

His message for those contemplating suicide, "Trust in God and don't give up. Read the Gospel according to St. John, Chapter 14. Christ said 'Love one another as I have loved you.'"

Asked if he would jump again, he said. "No. It's against God's law; 'thou shalt not kill.'"

- - - -

A 30-year-old San Francisco stock exchange employee became the ninth known survivor after his leap on February 8, 1975. He was taken to Marin General hospital where his

Donner

condition was reported as critical but stable.

- - - -

Tom McPherson, a 66-year-old retired longshoreman, was fishing at Fort Point early Friday morning on April 29, 1976. It was a fine day with a clear blue sky and bright sun. A perfect day for fishing. He cast his line into the choppy waters and was watching to see where it hit when he saw a form falling from the Bridge. He was "shaken up," but when he saw the person swimming and being carried out to sea by the tide, he quickly called to nearby fishermen to summon the Coast Guard. The other fishermen didn't think anything was wrong because all they saw was a young woman swimming.

"When you see people in distress you want to help them," said Tom, who ran to the entrance of old Fort Point where he told a National Park Service worker about the leaper. The worker called his boss, James McOwien. McOwien grabbed a life ring with a rope attached and the three ran back. After two tries McOwien reached the desperate swimmer, but she looked as if she was having a difficult time hanging on to the life ring.

"The only thing I could do was jump in after her," said the 43-year-old McOwien. "At a time like that you try to do the best you can. When I reached her she didn't say anything. That water was just too damn cold. I tied a rope around her, using a running bowline so the rope wouldn't tighten up around her chest. I was afraid she might have chest injuries."

The attractive young woman, in her early 20's, was hauled up on land suffering from shock, but with a good pulse. When she opened her eyes the first thing she said was "Keep talking to me." A few minutes later she said her lungs hurt and her eyes burned.

When an ambulance arrived medics asked her why she had jumped. Her answer was that she was seeing a psychiatrist and they would have to ask him. After investigating, police learned the woman had been living in a half-way house in The City where a spokesman said she had not talked of suicide nor seemed depressed.

At Letterman Hospital she was described as being in good condition with no serious injuries but suffering from hypothermia after being so long in the frigid waters. The woman's purse, left near the south tower where she stepped off the span, contained no suicide note nor anything of interest. She was the second woman among the ten survivors thus far.

- - - -

The 20-year-old had given The City a shock but on November 5, 1977, another female, this one still in her teens, sent another shudder through the Bay Area and rekindled calls for erecting a suicide barrier.

Two friends, a contractor and a baseball umpire, were cycling across the Bridge that morning when the contractor spotted a teenage girl standing on the cat-walk the other side of the railing about 30 yards north of the south tower. He pulled his bike along side and shouted, "Hey, come over here, I want to talk to you." The girl shook her head, and as the two cyclists dropped their bikes and made a dash to reach her, she nonchalantly looked down at the water for a second, held her nose and jumped.

A boater from Hayward was passing under the Bridge in his 16-foot outboard motorboat and saw the girl splash not 30 yards in front of him. When he and his companions lifted her out of the water she cried, "Let me die." She was transferred

Donner

to a Coast Guard boat and rushed by ambulance to Letterman Hospital within 13 minutes of her leap. She sustained internal injuries but was otherwise in fair condition. She had been wearing hiking boots.

The eleventh survivor had been living in a home for girls in The City but had moved back with her parents. Two weeks previously she asked to return to the girls' home.

- - - -

There is a saying about good things coming in threes (as well as disasters), and for a 26-year-old San Francisco secretary at a printing company, being the third woman to survive a Bridge leap was certainly a charm.

For two brothers, however, Allen Carter, 35, of San Jose and Wes Carter, 37, visiting from New Hampshire, their trip to The City and Fort Point turned into a more memorable occasion than they had planned.

Late in the afternoon of March 15, 1978, as the two brothers were strolling around to the water side of Fort Point, they saw a woman bobbing in the waves some 30 yards from the concrete abutment, drifting slowly out to sea. They leaped into the water as other witnesses threw them a life ring, which they pulled out to the struggling woman. By the time a Coast Guard boat reached the three, they had drifted 200 yards seaward. When crewmen pulled the young lady onto the boat she was grinning. They quickly administered oxygen and wrapped the three in blankets to treat them for hypothermia.

She was not only the third woman of twelve survivors but the third person within 24 hours to leap from the Bridge. People on a sightseeing boat reported a man's body in the water near the south tower, and several hours before the young woman jumped, motorists reported seeing a man in his early 20's jump from the east side near the south tower. The two bodies were not recovered.

- - - -

On December 21, 1978, two people jumped from the east side near the south tower, a favorite spot because of its quick and easy access. One was a woman in her mid-20's, the other, a man also in his mid-20's. The woman survived, rescued by the Coast Guard and was rushed to Letterman Hospital. The body of the man was found a quarter of a mile west of the Bridge. The two had jumped within two hours of each other, before noon. She was the fourth woman in a row to join the 13 known survivors.

- - - -

The string of women survivors continued with the 14th survivor, a 25-year-old who landed in the moat around the south tower on September 12, 1979. When the Coast Guard crew pulled her from inside the moat, they thought she was dead because she was badly bruised and unconscious. But then they saw her leg move and heard her call, "Help me, I'm falling. I'm hurt."

While bringing her back to Fort Point and a waiting ambulance, she was asked why such a pretty woman would want to commit suicide. She responded, "I don't know. I don't know." She was taken to the hospital where she underwent extensive surgery and was listed in poor condition.

- - - -

It is no accident that the majority of survivors were young. Their greater physical stamina and resilience certainly puts the odds of survival more in their favor than older leapers. This was especially true of the 15th survivor who came through the ordeal with hardly a scratch and even swam ashore. What scars were on his psyche is another matter.

Donner

Doctors described the 17-year-old San Anselmo youth as being in "excellent physical shape, one of the healthiest young people I've ever seen. He must have hit the water just right on his rear end or lower back, then slipped right under the water."

On December 19, 1979, a Bridge paint foreman was working near the south tower at 1:30 p.m. when he noticed the lad pacing back and forth, whistling as though he hadn't a care in the world.

"He kept walking there for about a half hour and I got suspicious when he kept looking around at me," said the foreman.

Suddenly the young man took off his jacket, handed it to a young passerby saying, "Give this to my mother." Then he sprang over the rail, plunged the 220 feet and landed some 50 yards north of Fort Point.

A Park Ranger working at Fort Point heard Bridgeworkers shouting from above and spotted the young man swimming toward him. He threw out a lifeline and pulled him ashore. Despite the fall and tough 100-yard swim through a heavy current, the teenager walked up the beach to Fort Point where he was wrapped in blankets and put in front of a fireplace to await an ambulance.

"His clothes were shredded from the fall," said the Ranger.

The boy's teachers and friends at the high school, where he played the grueling sport of water polo and was also a gymnast, were stunned by the news. Friends described him as likable but self-absorbed. "He has a lot of friends and talks to you but keeps his feelings to himself," they said. "Lots of girls like him, he's real popular, but real modest."

"I was with him just before he jumped," said his friend of 15 years. "He seemed in good spirits. He didn't show anything. I'm as much in awe of this as anybody. I don't think anybody knows why but him."

A doctor at the hospital said the youth remembered coming to the Bridge but recalled nothing about his leap. As of this date 696 others known to have jumped were less fortunate.

- - - -

The 16th survivor statistic occurred on June 3, 1984, a man from Oakland. The 17th was a man from Tracy who jumped August 21, 1985, and the 18th was another teen from Marin county, who jumped the following year.

The 19th person to "jump and tell" was one of those rare Bridge "statistics" who came from out of state. The 24-year-old man hailed from Providence, Utah. Whether the Bridge was his planned destination is not known. On April 19, 1990, he was already the sixth person to jump from the Bridge that year. Two iron workers spotted the young man as he gazed out to the Pacific on the west side of the span shortly before noon.

As the iron workers kept a wary eye on the lad, he suddenly twirled around and dashed across the six lanes narrowly avoiding being hit by a pickup truck. Without pausing, he climbed over the railing and clung to the steel bracing under the Bridge. For the next 15 minutes the iron workers and police tried to talk him out of letting go, but he shouted at them to leave him alone, and that he "wanted to talk to his psychiatrist." He finally let go and dropped to the channel where a waiting Coast Guard boat quickly retrieved him. He was taken to Marin General Hospital where he was reported in grave condition.

Donner

There have been a few other survivors recorded but those died within hours of their jumps.

A San Francisco psychiatrist, who interviewed seven of the earliest survivors, said they consistently recalled feelings of transcendence and spiritual rebirth during their falls. One survivor said, "I felt like a bird flying, total relief. In my mind I was getting away from one realm and into another. Even now, while I'm still symbolically looking for the better world, I'm still in that place between the Bridge and the water."

Five survivors said if they could not have jumped from the Golden Gate Bridge, they would not have tried to commit suicide, backing the argument of those who had been calling for barriers on the span.

The survivors provided glimpses of fantastic emotions passing through their minds during the four-second fall, sensations of peace, dreaming, relief and even ecstasy. Only one recalled moving swiftly through the air. Another said it was a good feeling with no screaming. "It was the most pleasant feeling I ever had," he said. Two of the seven, subsequently attempted suicide again. The rest had supposedly eliminated suicide from their thoughts.

None recalled having their lives flash before them, a phenomenon widely reported by those who have had close calls with death. Five reported blacking out before hitting the water and two clearly remembered the impact going in feet first. An autopsy of 169 Bridge suicides found that only eight persons drowned while the rest died because of injuries. (See Rescuers Chapter).

Chapter Five:

Those Who Tried and Failed

Many have attempted to commit suicide from the Golden Gate Bridge, but for strange--and often seemingly miraculous reasons--their lives were spared. One spent the night suspended 260 feet over the swirling channel nearly bleeding from self-inflicted wounds. Others leaped but somehow wound up on girders under the roadway and teetered for minutes or hours, between this life and the next. One was saved by the very rope he thought to hang himself from a girder.

For two privates on a short furlough from the Army before being shipped overseas, their first walk across the fabled Golden Gate Bridge was indeed a memorable one. It was October 11, 1941, and they decided to get an early sight-seeing start. They had a quick breakfast, then took a cab to the south end of the Bridge and walked the entire span to Vista Point on the Marin side, stopping often to take in the breathtaking views. They were on their way back and had just passed the south tower on the east side when they heard a man yelling for help. They looked around but saw no one then realized the shouts were coming from under the Bridge. They dashed to the Toll Plaza and notified a CHP sergeant who immediately alerted the Coast Guard and summoned police and fire department rescue squads.

Another CHP officer sped to where the soldiers indicated they heard the calls and started shouting. When he located the answering yells, he climbed the railing and crawled warily down to the main girder where he saw a man perched on a narrow beam.

"How long have you been here," the officer shouted.

"Since yesterday," the man answered.

The 39-year-old San Franciscan had started his grim saga a little after 4 p.m. the preceding day and lay suspended between sky and sea, buffeted by the frigid winds funneling through the Gate for more than 16 hours. He told the officer he had climbed over the railing to leap to his death but had slipped and landed on the outside girder. From there he edged backward onto the crossbeam. Sometime during the long night he took out his knife and slashed his wrists and throat.

The rescue team's first try was to tie a rope around the waist of one officer and lower him over the side, but this was quickly abandoned as too risky. Then riggers created a pallet with a long plank and some rope. As a Coast Guard boat circled the waters below, the would-be suicide was gingerly hauled to safety on the plank. As he was nearing the roadway he admonished, "Be careful boys, don't drop me."

The first officer to reach the man said he had lost a lot of blood and was severely injured on his crawl to the girder. "There wasn't much skin left on his arms and hands and his fingernails were bent clear back or torn off completely," he reported. "He could barely talk. He had the strength to get where he was but wasn't strong enough after spending the night to crawl out."

Luckily no bones were broken in his fall. Had he passed out during his terrifying vigil, he would almost certainly have plunged to what he thought was a desired end. During his recuperation he sent a thank-you note to the police which, they said, "was one of the few they ever received."

- - - -

Donner

A 42-year-old mother who worked as a bank secretary in the South Bay was another "miraculous save." Divorced for six years, she had been dating a man for the past five years and was to be married in a few days. Then she received a letter with the shocking news: her "beau" was marrying another woman.

That's when the headaches started, headaches so severe she had blacked out a few times. On December 20, 1950, she had taken some Christmas presents to friends in Marin County and was driving back across the Bridge on her way home. She stopped the car about 100 feet beyond the south tower-- another minute and she would have been at the Toll Plaza. She got out and started to climb the railing on the ocean side as two Greyhound drivers, whose buses were empty, and a captain of the Bridge's security force saw her. All three slammed on their brakes and dashed to the railing to stop the woman. One reached for her arm but was too late to grab hold. Instead of falling 220 feet the woman landed on the steel girder five feet down and hung there precariously.

The three men quickly went over the railing to attempt to rescue her. One reached the girder where the woman lay, either dazed or unconscious. Passersby summoned a highway patrolman who brought a rope. The rescuers gingerly managed to get the rope around the woman's body, hoping all the while she wouldn't move and drop to certain death. Once the rope was secured they hauled her to safety where she told them she had lost consciousness and didn't know where she was or how she got there.

Police found four notes in her auto, one addressed "To Whom It May Concern" read: "I have a feeling something is going to happen to me and whatever it is will have been done by (man's name), may he pay in full."

The woman was taken to Emergency Hospital where she was comforted by her children. On this date, December 20, 1950, the official Bridge suicide toll was 116 with only one survivor, the 22-year-old woman who jumped in 1941.

- - - -

There have been numerous Good Samaritan stories involving would-be suicides from the Bridge, but one of the scariest involved Joe, a phone company cable splicer. He and his wife Kathy were driving back across the Bridge to their home in Marin County around 9 a.m., on February 8, 1952, and were just past mid-span when Joe saw a young man hanging a sports jacket on one of the nubbins on the railing. He slammed on the brakes and tore out of the car.

"I was really flying but I couldn't see the fellow," he recounted. "All of a sudden I saw his hand sliding along the rail, as though he was taking his time walking along the beam below, kind of picking out a place."

Joe grabbed the man's wrist and jerked him against the railing. As he reached over to get a firmer hold on the man, his feet left the ground as his body bent in an inverted U over the railing. Kathy saw what was happening and shrieked thinking her husband was going over head first.

Joe was huskier than the would-be leaper and felt he could have hauled him over the railing. His adrenaline had kicked in and he felt a tremendous surge of strength. But he didn't want to take the chance, thinking the man might pry loose and jump.

He kept telling me, "You're happily married, aren't you? Well, just leave me alone. Everything will be all right."

As this life and death tug-of-war was going on, Kathy was frantically trying to flag down traffic but there were only a few cars and none would stop. Finally a woman said she would send help.

Meanwhile Joe hung on, trying to talk the man out of jumping. After several minutes another car stopped, and a man came over to help Joe pull the fellow up and over the rail to safety. By that time a CHP officer arrived and took the young man away.

"I never knew I could hold anyone who struggled as hard as this guy did," said Joe, who admitted that after it was all over "my legs went wobbly."

His wife, Kathy, commented, "When I saw Joe almost go over the railing, I almost had a heart attack."

- - - -

The odds of success for another Good Samaritan who almost went down with a would-be suicide, were almost too great to calculate. It was around 4:30 a.m. on November 8, 1952, when a cement mixer truck driver was heading across the Bridge toward Marin County. He was getting a very early start for what was going to be a long day and had no idea it would start so dramatically. There was virtually no traffic and the Bridge was bathed in an eerie yellow cast from the sodium vapor lamps.

As he neared the north tower the truck driver saw the parked car and then a man standing on a girder looking as though bracing himself to jump. Without hesitation the driver braked his heavy rig to a stop and ran to the railing. He grabbed the 38-year-old San Francisco paint salesman before he could jump and hung on though the man struggled violently. It is not known how long this struggle lasted or what the two men said during this time, but the driver must have felt his strength giving away because he started yelling for help.

Miraculously, a cab driver from Concord, an East Bay

suburb, was driving to Hamilton Air Force Base in Marin County with two enlisted men. They saw the parked cement truck, heard the calls for help and clamored out of the cab. With the reinforcements they were able to haul the paint salesman to safety. The would-be leaper told CHP officers he had a quarrel with his wife and became despondent. He was taken to a San Francisco hospital for observation.

After the officers arrived the cement truck driver got into his rig and drove off. No one asked his name or where he was from.

- - - -

A San Francisco freelance photographer beat the odds on May 12, 1952, for twice being in the right place at the right time regarding Bridge dramas.

The first time was less than a month previous when a passing motorist tried to prevent a 61-year-old San Francisco society matron from jumping off near the north tower. The photographer was taking photos of passing ships when the drama occurred. A San Anselmo motorist saw the woman standing on the ledge outside the east railing and stopped his car. He dashed over to the woman and pleaded with her not to jump. The woman said she had an incurable illness, but the motorist insisted there were doctors who could cure her. The photographer snapped several photos while this dialogue was taking place. As the motorist tried to coax the woman to come closer so he could grab on to her, she just let go. Her body was recovered by the Coast Guard. She was the fourth suicide in as many days from the Bridge.

On this particular day, however, the circumstances would not be as grim.

Rita, a young San Francisco wife, had another squabble with her husband, the third big blowup in as many weeks, and she felt tired, depressed and exhausted. Only 21, the slender and attractive young lady had two children, a boy, 2 1/2-years-old and a girl, just four months. When her husband left that morning, after another spate of angry words, she made breakfast for the children and sat listlessly watching them play with their plastic toys on the floor. Around 11 she got the children dressed, bundled them into the family Pontiac and drove to the Bridge.

She passed through the Toll Plaza and parked in mid-span. The photographer, who was there again to take photos of passing ships, spotted the car stop along the east walkway. A Bridge security officer just happened to be walking near that point at exactly the same time. When the photographer saw the woman get out of the car and start to climb the railing he shouted to the officer and sprinted toward them.

"We ran up to her together," said the photographer, "and the officer grabbed her. She was struggling and crying and said, 'Let me go, let me go.' She was fighting him tooth and nail all the way. When I saw that the officer had a good hold on her, I stepped back to take some photos."

After the woman was subdued, they found the two children in the car with the older boy sobbing, "Mommie's going away"

The young mother and her babies were taken to the Toll Plaza where officers called the woman's husband who took the family home.

- - -

Marin County commuters must have thought a convention was taking place on the Bridge the morning of March 3, 1993, when about 20 officers and maintenance men became involved in the rescue of a 26-year-old Los Angeles man.

The drama started when workers saw the man walking on the ocean side of the Bridge and told him the walkway was closed until 5 a.m. He was dressed in a business suit and trench coat, but at that point he took off his dress shoes and put on a pair of sneakers. Then he calmly climbed over the rail and onto the steel catwalk known as the "chord," an enginering term, near the middle of the span. As officers sped to the scene, traffic was halted. The young man had a 15-foot length of rope tied around his neck and kept would-be rescuers away with a five-inch, serrated knife.

For several hours they tried to talk him out of jumping. An officer with the San Francisco Psychiatric Unit was summoned and spent several more hours trying to reason with the man.

"It was like talking to a brick wall," said the officer. "In my experience most of the people talk to you; they're crying, they're upset. It's a real good sign when they engage with you. This person wouldn't engage with anyone. He wouldn't even look anyone in the eye."

The team of rescuers recoiled in horror when the young man jumped from his perch. However, fate intervened and the rope around his neck caught on a cable. Bridge workers quickly pulled him to safety where he was resuscitated.

"I can't believe he did this in front of me," said the astounded officer from the psychiatric unit. When the officer visited the man in the hospital the would-be suicide thanked him for talking to him and apologized for causing the mammoth traffic jam.

- - - -

Another chap also perched on a girder in the substructure of the span, threatening to jump if the CHP officer came any closer. Using psychology, the officer immediately drew his gun and told the man if he didn't come back up he'd shoot. The fellow came up at once not realizing the irony of the situation until he was safe and glad he hadn't taken the fatal plunge.

There was another occasion when an officer used reverse psychology on a man who threatened to jump. "Awe, go ahead and jump. Who cares?" said the officer hoping the man would change his mind. He didn't.

One save proved rather costly in terms of an auto pileup. Just after midnight on September 4, 1968, a San Mateo woman stopped her northbound car in mid-span and ran to the east railing. A visitor from Manila saw what was happening and stopped his car immediately behind the woman's, jumped out and was able to grab one leg as she was climbing over. During the ensuing struggle a third vehicle smashed into the visitor's car, and then two more joined the pileup. The driver of the last car was the most seriously hurt and had to be taken to Marin General hospital. The lady was saved and escorted off the Bridge by CHP. The wrecks took longer to remove.

Through the years there have been a number of indecisive would-be leapers who spent a night of terror, suffering the bone-chilling fog while clinging to a girder under the Bridge. This case involved an attractive 31-year-old speech therapist from San Francisco, who crawled under the span at about 3 p.m. July 7, 1969. A motorist reported seeing her but when officers went to check they found nothing. She had hidden from view. At 7:45 a.m. the next day another call came in, and this time officers located the woman.

The two officers climbed down toward her but backed off when she threatened to jump and shouted at them, "My life is ruined. I'm insane. I'm out of my mind. I really want to die." Five maintenance men joined in the rescue by climbing along the deck from the opposite side. When they got within eight feet of her, she again threatened to jump, shifting her body closer to the perilous 260 foot drop.

While officers engaged her in conversation, the maintenance workers skillfully moved a portable net beneath her and slowly began to surround her. When one officer tried to throw a rope to her, one of her hands slipped and she almost fell. When the men grabbed her, she fought violently, screaming and weeping all the while. One rescuer suffered a bite on the hand for his courageous effort. The woman was taken to a psychiatric ward in The City.

- - - -

People kept asking how it was possible for a 33-year-old Army sergeant to walk out of psychiatric ward at Letterman clad only in blue hospital pajamas and onto the Bridge without being noticed. But he did, one blustery, winter day, crawling over the railing somehow getting to "the one spot on the Bridge where there's no way to get at him," said Bridge authorities. The spot was near the Fort Point arch, 180 feet above ground, where for four bitterly cold and agonizing hours the man listened to pleas to come down from his perch.

"I got nothing to live for. I got no home. I got no wife. If I don't go now I'll go some other time. So why not now," he shouted at rescuers over the sound of the wind whistling through the Bridge rigging.

Army psychiatrists, who were summoned to help, said the man's emotional troubles apparently originated when his wife left him some years before. A chaplain also came to assist in talking the man out of his threat.

Meanwhile, San Francisco firemen arrived at the scene and began setting up nets on the ground to catch the sergeant if he fell or jumped. An Army ambulance was also moved into a nearby position as well as a Coast Guard patrol boat in case the wind blew him into the water.

Sightseers had to be kept moving, and a dozen reporters and photographers were kept out of sight for fear their presence might trigger the man's threatened jump.

At the end of the four hours the six-foot sergeant finally came down, shaking uncontrollably from exposure to the cold. But as he was lead to a waiting ambulance he kept muttering, "I should have jumped. I should have jumped dozens of times."

- - - -

While many have leaped from the span's roadway or from girders beneath, few have had the daring to crawl up the suspension cable to the top of the 740-foot towers. An unemployed carpenter did just that on January 21, 1971, after riding his bike to the Bridge. The early afternoon traffic jammed, and sightseers congregated to watch as the daredevil swung around on the safety cables of the south tower, using them like parallel bars.

Officers and Bridge workers took the tower elevator to the top and approached the man, offering him a safety belt. He grabbed it and flung it into the Bay. While talking with him rescuers learned he was distraught because his wife left him taking their two children. He was concerned about them and wanted to see them. When workers offered him a safety belt the second time, he appeared "cooled off," took the device and was led to safety.

It was a busy day on the Bridge that particular day with two other potential suicides being prevented. At 9:20 a.m. officers stopped a 58-year-old San Francisco woman who was acting suspiciously. She told them she had planned to jump. Just before noon, a 43-year-old woman was stopped and

Donner

questioned when she was "obviously planning to jump," said officers.

Another young man attempted the same tower feat when he parked his car near the south tower and methodically climbed along the cable to the top of the 740-foot structure. Again, Bridge workers, who by this time, were receiving special training in how to save would-be suicides, took the elevator to the top of the tower, and, after two hours, were able to persuade the man to come down.

Donner

Chapter Six:

Fathers and Their Children

After straining his back while repairing an elevator, Bertrand (not his real name) was never quite the same. It seemed one thing after another continued to batter the 33-year-old's life like a series of storms slamming the coast. He was in constant pain for the past six months despite the medication, and now doctors said there was something wrong with his heart. This last bit of news was almost too much to bear and left him moody and despondent.

He was still able to work but planned to take two weeks off in July for a vacation to the Redwoods up north, in Sonoma County. Shortly after breakfast on July 23, 1945, Bertrand headed to the garage of the family home in San Francisco, telling his wife he was going to a nearby gas station to fill up the tank for the coming trip. He paused at the door saying, "I think I'll go to the doctor's too, and take Lynn with me. She can wait outside." He was seeing a heart doctor and went for periodic checkups. Both his wife and mother-in-law protested about leaving the five-year-old in the car while he was in the doctor's office. "OK," he relented, "I'll take her inside with me."

Bertrand and his wife had two children, eight-year-old Sissy, who was not feeling well and stayed in bed that day, and blond, curly-haired, Lynn, who was Bertrand's favorite. Lynn was told to get a sweater because it was still a bit chilly. Bertrand and his daughter climbed into the family car and drove off as Lynn waved good-bye to her mother. They never went to the doctor's.

Bertrand drove to a nearby gas station but only bought two dollars worth of gas. Then he drove toward the Golden Gate Bridge. Present day traffic at 8:30 a.m. would still be heavy but in 1945 there were fewer autos and even less commuting. Also, in today's traffic, regardless of the hour, a car stopped on the Bridge would trigger a quick response from the CHP. On that morning, however, Bertrand stopped the car about 30 yards past the south tower and parked.

Two riggers working on the Bridge observed what was going on. One said he saw a little girl get out of the car and walk to the railing. Another also reported seeing a little blond girl standing by the railing alone.

"When I glanced again I saw her climbing the railing onto the girder below. She leaped off the girder, and it wasn't until her body was in the water that I saw a man come out of the car."

The other eyewitness reported seeing "the little girl fall past me and land flat on the water."

Seconds after Lynn jumped her father dashed to the railing, looked down and saw her body. He pulled himself to the top of the railing and "made a perfect dive as though he were a professional swimmer," said both witnesses.

The riggers saw the two bodies floating, but a swift tide quickly carried them seaward. Although rescue boats searched for hours, father and daughter were never seen again.

It was the first time since the Bridge opened that a tragedy like this occurred. Lynn became the youngest person to die leaping from the Bridge. Unfortunately, that would change.

When told of the incident, Bertrand's wife sobbed, "I knew it. I knew it."

On the front seat of Bertrand's car police found a wallet with $1.57 in it, and a note that simply said: "I and my daughter committed suicide." Authorities remained forever baffled over how the father could have persuaded his little daughter to commit such a bold and desperate act. Lynn would have been six years old in two weeks.

- - - - - -

His neighbors, friends and fellow workers described Andrew, 32, as a loving father and reliable employee.

"He was a nice man, very mild-mannered and he loved kids," said a neighbor whose own son often went on bicycle trips with Andrew and his 11-year-old stepson.

Andrew and his wife, Pat, 37, had been married for four-and-a-half years, and had a three-year-old girl, Sally. They had lived in their house in the suburbs for three years, but seven months earlier their lives changed dramatically. Although no one could recall the couple squabbling or any raging outbursts, Pat decided to end the marriage. Even though the divorce was final the couple remained on good terms, with Andrew coming over to take care of the children when his ex-wife went out on a date.

Over the holidays they tried to patch things up as Andrew moved back with his ex-wife. It didn't work out, and he returned to his apartment a few blocks away.

On Friday, January 29, 1993, Andrew had arranged to take the day off so he could take Sally for an outing to The City while Pat worked. Pat's 11-year-old son was in school. Father and daughter went off in his silver BMW and drove around for a while. At noon he stopped to make a phone call to his ex-mother-in-law asking her to pick up Pat's son after school.

Donner

It was a beautiful day, one of those balmy winter days that are milder than summer days when the fog often rolls in. Andrew parked the car at the south end of the Bridge, and the pair joined the tourists taking advantage of the favorable weather. About a third of the way to mid-span Sally was having a hard time keeping up with her father so Andrew scooped her up and put her on his shoulders. They walked with the other sightseers looking out over the blue San Francisco Bay toward Alcatraz and Angel Island.

The Bridge's security chief drove by during a routine check, saw Andrew walking along, bouncing the little girl on his shoulders and thought they were just part of the crowd of tourists enjoying the fabulous view and fantastic day. When he got to the Toll Plaza, however, an ironworker had already reported that a man carrying a small child was behaving strangely. As the security officer pulled up, the maintenance men and dozens of tourists watched in horror as Andrew suddenly hurled Sally over the railing, and before anyone could reach him, leaped over himself. The entire drama was captured on the Bridge's closed circuit TV.

The Coast Guard rescue crew raced to the Marin side of the channel where they pulled father and daughter from the chilly water at 2:34 p.m. Andrew was pronounced dead at the hospital. A medical team tried for 45 minutes to revive little Sally but she died at 3:55 p.m., the youngest to be killed from a Bridge leap. This, also, was soon to change.

When police opened the truck of Andrew's car they found a box of shells and a 12 gauge semi-automatic shotgun with three rounds of ammunition still in it. When Pat's mother brought her grandson home from school, she found her daughter lying in a pool of blood, dead from a shotgun blast in the mouth. There was a note from Andrew to the 11-year-old saying

Donner

he was sorry for what he had done and was about to do. The note also said Andrew was leaving all his possessions to the boy, who later returned to live with his natural father in another state.

- - - -

Fred and his two-year-old son, Mark, were spending the Thanksgiving holiday in 1993 with relatives. He was trying to have a good time, but his thoughts were constantly drifting back to his pending divorce and custody fight. He and his wife of more than three years had broken up two months previously but tried to maintain civil relations. She was out of town this day, with her son by a previous marriage, celebrating the holiday with her own family.

Fred tried to "put on a happy face" while playing with his young son and watching TV with his cousins. The subject of football and the Forty Niners dominated the conversation at the beginning of the feast but splintered into several conversations later. There was more than enough food and after several helpings of turkey and huge helpings of other food, there was the usual talk about not eating for a month or going for a long walk. It was nearing 4 p.m. and Fred started to make moves to go, saying he had some things to take care of. He helped little Mark get into his jump suit and searched for the tyke's tiny blue sneakers. After hugs and "thanks," Fred and his son drove away. Instead of heading home, however, he drove to the Bridge.

At 5 p.m. it was already dusk and the Bridge's distinctive yellow sodium vapor lamps were turned on. Fred parked at the south end, put Mark in the baby stroller he took from the trunk and started walking. Being Thanksgiving there was little traffic at that time and even fewer pedestrians. Things might have ended differently, if there had been, since a single man pushing a baby stroller along the span at that time of day would have seemed unusual.

A CHP officer at the Toll Plaza received a call just after 5 p.m. alerting him to "a man pushing a stroller acting peculiar." Before he could get out the door another call came in. This was from a Bridge tow truck operator who reported he just saw a man with a child in his arms leap from the east side of the span. The officer got into his patrol car and sped to the location. All he found was an empty stroller.

With his binoculars the officer scanned the darkening scene below and spotted the two bodies about 50 feet apart. A Coast Guard boat was already speeding to the scene. The crew spotted the child's body, but it sank before they could get to it. They recovered the father's body but were unable to revive him. Spotlights from a helicopter and two Coast Guard ships criss-crossed the now blackened waters for several hours before the search for baby Mark was called off.

- - - -

Patrick Murphy, Sr. (not his real name) was a credit manager at a San Jose hardware firm. Just before closing time he was told that auditors would make a routine check of his books. When he left work that day, September 27, 1954, he got into his 1953 Pontiac but instead of driving home to his family, he headed toward San Francisco and the Bridge. He drove through the Toll Plaza, crossed the span and parked at Vista Point on the north end. Then he walked calmly back out to the middle of the span on the east side and jumped to his death.

Five days later, on October 1, the same 1953 Pontiac again passed through the Toll Plaza only this time it stopped midway on the Bridge and a 24-year-old pre-med student got out, calmly walked to the railing and leaped to his death.

Donner

His name was Patrick Murphy, Jr. Patrolmen found his wallet on the seat of the car and an unsigned note stating: "I want to keep Dad company." Father and son became the 140th and 141st known suicides from the Bridge.

Donner

Chapter Seven:

Couples

According to official reports, the first double death leap from the Golden Gate Bridge occurred October 2, 1977, 40 years after the Bridge opened.

On that date a young Asian man and woman jumped from the span directly beneath the north tower and landed on the pavement of Lime Point Road about 20 feet from the rocky shoreline. Police speculated the couple had walked from Vista Point at the north end of the Bridge although no vehicle was found abandoned. Neither body had any identifying papers, but police gave a detailed description of what the two were wearing hoping someone would come forth to identify them. The tragic couple became the 612th and 613th persons to die jumping off the Bridge.

- - - -

Conrad, a 26-year-old male nurse, had been worried about finding a job. He wanted to get his mind off his problems so he decided to go for an outing to Sausalito, his favorite place in Marin County just across the Bridge. The weather there in the "banana belt" seemed always sunny and warm. He phoned his friend Rita, also a nurse, to join him and picked her up at her apartment near the Mission District.

The date was June 10, 1940, as the pair drove over the Bridge and into sun-splashed Sausalito. They moseyed around the docks gazing at the fancy sailboats, then went over to Lippert's for ice cream cones. Though Conrad still indicated concern about his job prospects, Rita thought his spirits had picked up a little. They were on their way back across the Bridge when he suddenly stopped the car in mid-span, got out and hurtled over the ocean-side railing, leaving his companion in a state of shock.

As CHP officers were questioning the young lady, a motorist pulled up and said he had just seen a woman jump from the span on the east side. When police arrived at the scene they found a purse with identification papers belonging to a 36-year-old Stockton woman who had recently suffered a nervous collapse. A letter to her father said she was "unable to face unspeakable suffering."

- - - -

George and Eve, a middle-aged couple who lived in Berkeley, had been arguing bitterly for several months over his drinking problem. He couldn't explain it but he started drinking heavily about a year ago and it just kept getting worse. The last straw for his wife was when he was told to leave the accounting firm where he worked and get help with his problem. The bickering intensified after that.

On August 29, 1945, they had driven to Marin County and now, a little before 4 p.m., were crossing the Bridge to visit a relative in The City. An argument that started earlier was continuing. In mid-span Eve shouted, "I can't stand this any longer. Stop the car, I'm getting out." George stopped the car and, according to witnesses, calmly watched his wife get out, climb over the railing and jump. Witnesses quoted George as saying, "To hell with her. Let her go," and drove off, but not before one witness took down the license plate number.

When police finally located George to identify the body they asked him why he didn't stop his wife from jumping.

"What could I do?" he mumbled. "We had been quarreling. It came to an end yesterday on the Bridge. For some reason I just drove away. I don't know why."

When he saw the body of his wife at the morgue, he bent over, kissed her forehead and burst into bitter sobs.

- - - -

Two buddies, Allen, 32, and Stan, 40, shared more than an interest in sports--they both were having girl problems. On May 2, 1952, they were in their favorite local pub in The City commiserating with each other and sucking up a lot of suds. Around midnight, Allen turned to his buddy and said, "If you've got the guts, let's go for a swim." They shook hands on it then called a cab and told the driver to take them to the north side of the Bridge. When the cab reached mid-span, Allen told the driver to stop, handing him his wallet and $5. The two buddies got out as the cabby drove on. They teetered over to the railing and Allen started climbing over it. A passing motorist saw them and notified authorities when he went through the Toll Plaza.

As CHP officers pulled up, Allen shouted, "You cops ain't gonna take me," and in an instant was over the side, streaking toward the channel. The officers managed to grab Stan by the leg as he tried to join his pal, and dragged him to safety. Later that night the cabby turned in Allen's wallet at a San Francisco police station, saying he thought his pal was going to sober him up by walking to the Marin side of the Bridge.

- - - -

Sam and Josie, who were making plans to be married, had been going "steady" for the past two years and like many couples had their share of spats including some within the past few days. On October 15, 1972, they had decided to go

Donner

for a drive to Marin County. They were on their way back late in the afternoon, southbound over the Bridge when the 36-year-old man stopped the car in mid-span. He leaned over, murmured "I love you," and kissed his fiancee. Then he got out of the car and leaped over the railing to become the Bridge's 460th known suicide.

- - - -

Though these events did not involve a couple, it was unusual in that within a two hour time frame one young man jumped to his death from the Bay Bridge while an ailing World War II veteran took his life off the Golden Gate. The date was August 1, 1952, when a 22-year-old UC Davis student plunged from the Bay Bridge after slashing himself earlier with a razor. At the cabin where he was living, investigators found a message scrawled in blood on the floor: "People are no damn good." The veteran, whose body landed on a Crissy field road in the Presidio, had been hospitalized for more than a year.

- - - -

A history-making event occurred on the Bridge when two men leaped to their deaths within three hours of each other on October 23, 1969. A CHP captain, who had worked on the Bridge for all but two of its 32 years, at that time said he couldn't recall an incident like it.

A strange twist to this event was that two television crews were on the Bridge that very day, one from CBS' "60 Minutes," the other from KPIX-TV, a local station, doing separate documentaries on the graceful span's lure for people bent on taking their lives. Neither crew was in position to capture the death leaps on film.

The first victim, a Sacramento man, parked his car at Vista Point on the north side of the span, and walked back along the east side to the north tower. He jumped at 11:44 a.m. His body was recovered by two men on an inbound fishing boat. The second man, a 68-year-old San Franciscan, jumped at 1:58 p.m., with the Coast Guard recovering the body 17 minutes later. The men were the 368th and 369th known suicides from the Bridge.

The irony of the historic two suicides in one day was that they took place during a year in which specially trained roving patrols were initiated to thwart would-be leapers and had been proving effective. In the first six months of 1969 only five people died leaping from the Bridge whereas the average for the same period during the previous five-years was 13. Fifty-two people were prevented from jumping during the first six months of 1969.

- - - -

It took 32 years to record the first double suicide in a single day from the Bridge but only two years to repeat that grim event. A man and woman jumped from the span December 5, 1971, and just three weeks later, on January 1, 1972, two men jumped within 35 minutes of each other becoming the 437th and 438th known suicides from the Golden Gate.

On December 22, 1978, a man and woman in their 20's jumped from the span in unrelated incidents. The woman survived, becoming the 12th person to do so while the man was not as fortunate. The Coast Guard recovered his body a mile west of the Bridge.

Two French tourists were strolling over the span during the morning of November 10, 1981, when they saw a man in midspan climb the railing and leap to his death. Less than two hours later two teen girls, one from Rhonert Park, north of San Francisco, and the other from Santa Rosa, were casually

Donner

walking along the Bridge on the east side when suddenly the 18-year-old from Rohnert Park without a word, quickly climbed the railing and jumped to her death. Her friend was unable to give a reason for the suicide. The two leapers became the 719th and 720th known suicides.

Donner

Chapter Eight:

Those Who Left Notes

Many suicides from the Golden Gate Bridge, starting with the very first one, left notes. There were no doubt more notes left by those entering dramatically into eternity but either they were not revealed by authorities, were not found, or were kept secret by relatives.

The 49-year-old World War I veteran made history by becoming the first person to leap from the Golden Gate Bridge on August 7, 1937, a little over two months after the span was officially opened. He was strolling along the east walkway with other pedestrians and reached the center at about 3:20 p.m. He removed his coat and started to climb the railing. He overcame the efforts of a passerby to restrain him and plunged to his death. His terse farewell note simply said: "This is where I get off."

Brief though it was, it may have inspired the 14th jumper not quite two years later, on March 27, 1939. Some observers thought he was part of the painting crew as he removed his coat and started scratching on the railing. But then he removed his shirt, quickly climbed over the railing and jumped. When a CHP sergeant investigated he saw this note scratched on the guard rail: "Here is where I go." The man left the nickel, perhaps his last, he used to scratch his note.

On April 4, 1940, a 25-year-old rice mill worker left this message: "Dear Mother and Dad; Please try to forgive me."

Donner

On November 3 of the same year, a 27-year-old hardware salesman left this accusatory message: "Dear Friends and Relatives: I don't feel like explaining because you have never understood me, so why? I am sorry I have to do it this way."

A 32-year-old truck driver kissed his wife goodbye and promised to be home early. Later that day, June 26, 1941, she received a special delivery letter from him which said: "This is the only decent thing I ever did." A Bridge security guard found the man's car parked at the north end of the Bridge with a flat tire. On the front seat were the man's wallet and the beginning of another note: "This is being written because I..." and stopped there. The wife, who was left with a two year-old daughter, said her husband had been worrying about finances.

A distinguished, white-haired gentlemen calmly took off his coat and hat and made the fatal leap on September 25, 1945, leaving this note: "Effie, You are the sweetest woman that ever lived. I can't go on any longer. Love, Ed."

On November 1, 1945, a 42-year-old San Francisco mother tried unsuccessfully to phone her former husband, calling him at work to say that she was going to the Bridge to jump off. Unable to talk to him personally she left that message. She then had several drinks at a bar at Chestnut and Pierce Streets and phoned for a taxi. At the Bridge Toll Plaza she tipped the cab driver and told him to wait with his meter running while she went out "to take a look." The cabby also got out, strolled around gazing at the Bridge and was stunned to see a body hurtling to the water. The woman had left her coat, hat and purse on the span with a note to her daughter: "Honey, I love you; please forgive me, C has finally driven me crazy. I have no place to go. Please help mom for my sake.

It could kill her. I'm sorry for what I'm doing to you and mom but I can't go on this way. Mother."

The 94th leaper, on March 12, 1948, a 31-year-old World War II veteran with 76 combat missions, was thought to be suffering from what was then called "war neurosis." He left simple instructions: " Please phone Mrs. W. and ask her to go up the hill and break the news to my wife."

On May 3 of that year, a young male domestic left this farewell: "I am taking this way out since I no longer have anything to live for. My sister and brother-in-law have taken my baby from me. Don't hold anything against my wife."

A retired construction worker, suffering from ill health, departed this life on January 4, 1949, with this: "Dearest Momma: You will be better off without me. You have been a good wife and mother. God bless you and the children. I am a coward and no good." He was the 110th suicide.

A logger from Willets bade goodbye on March 29, 1950, with these words: "Dear Jane, Our plans never would work out. I'm going to leave you. You keep your chin up."

It is not known what the content was, but a 23-year-old sailor gave a note to his pal while walking on the Bridge on April 4, 1950, saying, "Call this girl and tell her I jumped off the Bridge." He became number 124.

When Bridge workers arrived on the job the morning of November 15, 1950, they found a pair of pants near the south tower. In one of the pockets was a note to a woman in Seattle and a copy of a telegram. The note read: "My dearest, tonight I will not bother you anymore. I cannot live without you and my children. Not having you by my side and a prison sentence staring me in the face, I just can't go on. I'm sorry for the disgrace I brought on you and the children. Please forgive me for what I have done and am doing now." The telegram stated: "Case postponed Nov. 15 for hearing. Trial will be in Dec. Will send letter." The case the 32-year-old Los Angeles truck driver referred to was only a minor traffic charge. The Coast Guard abandoned the search for his body after several hours.

The last note of a 49-year-old woman from Berkeley read: "Darling, I'm sorry it has to be this way, but there seems to be no answer. I love you." The date was March 16, 1951.

A 39-year-old law associate suffering from ill health, didn't leave a note but told his wife, "I'll be back in two minutes to finish my coffee," as he took five children to school. It was his last cup of coffee as he joined the growing number of leapers on November 20th, 1953.

"The water will be much warmer than your love," said the note left by the unofficial 200th suicide victim from the Bridge, a 47-year-old former employee of the University of California at Berkeley. (The body was not found and the next leaper, a woman, became the official 200th). The note went on to say "I only wish I could figure some other way out but without work and no love from my wife, this is the only thing I know to do. At least this way I can give her a little more to live on. Goodbye (name of wife), good luck. You'll be better off without me."

When notified of her husband's death, the 64-year-old wife told police they had argued over changing their pet Chihuahua's sweater. The dog, Jigger, had a pink sweater for evening wear and a white sweater for daytime wear, the wife explained. She told police her husband got up from his chair while they were watching television and
said "I'm going away." The couple were reportedly deeply in debt. The date was September 27, 1954.

Few teen leapers, it seems, leave suicide notes. This

one was different. On July 16, 1957, officers, alerted by an observant motorist, found a 13-year-old San Francisco girl staring down at the channel waters on the east side and escorted her off the Bridge. The girl "wouldn't say anything, not a single thing," officers reported, but in her pocket was the following note: "Please understand, Mother and Dad...Don't grieve...I'm just trouble...It should never have come about that I was conceived...Just call it fate. Dr. (the name was torn off) will talk to you because he understood me, I guess...because I let him know me a little inside...I couldn't... If God wanted me to live he would have stopped this...I hope he will help you to be happy now...I'm sorry to do this to you...."

On April 22, 1968, a Bridge patrolman was heading south in his vehicle when he spotted a young woman in her late 20's walking erratically. He sped to the Toll Plaza, made a quick U-turn and headed north along the east side to where he had observed the woman. By the time he got to the location he found only a three-quarter length coat and a note to "Bill" left on the walkway. The note read in part "...you have given me the happiest times of my life. I am no longer able to take from you. I've got a big void in my life." The note was signed Dianne. The once beautiful woman was plucked from the Bay by the Coast Guard at 1:10 p.m. and brought to the morgue where she was listed as Jane Doe Number 5 with the name Dianne in quotes. She was the Bridge's 341st suicide.

He was described as "cheerful and pleasant" and a promising member of the faculty at Stanford, so his colleagues were non-plused to learn his car was abandoned on the Bridge and his body found hours later floating near Mile Rock. The 27-year-old British citizen left a note to "My darling Dorothy" which read: "I realize we can never be happy together but I still love you. God bless you." The recipient could offer no reason for the suicide.

On Christmas Eve 1970, a 23-year-old postal worker became number 407 and left this note: "This is my last selfish act." His close friend, a Thai waiter at Enrico's in The City, told friends he dreamed about his friend's death almost every night for several days. On New Year's Eve he became number 408 leaving this note: "This is my last selfish act."

San Francisco writer, Barnaby Conrad, in his book *Name Dropping*, published in 1992, related how a San Mateo friend left a note saying "I changed my mind half-way down." But Conrad said he kept getting postcards from various places around the world from this friend but was unsure which one was the hoax, the suicide or the postcards.

The son of a famous writer left this acerbic message: "Please notify my ex-wife, beautiful children, mother, bill collectors, and friends. I'll notify my father when I meet him in hell."

A twist to those who jumped and left notes are those who leave notes but don't jump. Known as "pseudocides" by professionals, there have been more than 30 of these found on or near the Bridge, including one from a San Francisco supervisor in the early 1940's. He was found later, selling Bibles in Texas.

Chapter Nine:

The Mysterious and Unusual

All jumps from the Golden Gate Bridge have been unusual in that the very act itself is extraordinary. However, some leaps, because of strange or mysterious circumstances, go even beyond that.

One year after the Bridge opened, an elderly retired San Francisco business woman and mother of a prominent eye doctor, hobbled with the aid of a cane onto the Bridge, carrying an old suitcase. When she got mid-way, she pulled herself agonizingly over the railing and plummeted to her death. The suitcase was empty except for a few papers that identified the victim.

Later that year a 30-year-old Swiss man drove his auto to midspan and parked. A passing motorist saw him get out, walk to the railing where he paused briefly and then vaulted over. The motorist raced to the Toll Plaza to report the incident but the Coast Guard searched in vain for his body. A roommate told investigators the man had saved thousands of dollars and planned to return to his native country, but when he was let go from his job, he started gambling and lost all his money. He was the ninth suicide from the Golden Gate.

A month later a 25-year-old Jewish bride of two weeks, who fled Germany and had been in the U.S. only three months, became the 10th confirmed suicide from the Bridge. She left a note to her husband saying she was sick at heart at the persecution of her relatives in Nazi Germany. "Life is without sense anymore," she concluded. Two fisherman were just below when she jumped, but because of the thick fog weren't sure what they had seen until the body came to the surface.

One week before, an early security patrol spotted a familiar face on the Bridge, a 28-year-old hotel maid who had been turned over to police the week before when they suspected she intended to jump. The first time she said she was just taking a walk to think out her problem of why the other maids at the hotel didn't like her. When she was escorted off the second time she said, "The Bridge will be here a long time. Some day I will be able to get past you and jump."

In February 1940, a 21-year-old blond model was driving across the Bridge near midnight from San Francisco when she made a U-turn and headed back. Her car was found parked in the middle of the span with a note on the front seat stating: "This isn't done for self-pity, love or revenge. I am simply doing a very good deed. Please notify Mrs.(name)," and was signed Phyllis.

When police tried to put the pieces together they learned the young woman was an orphan, and was having difficulty earning a living after the death of her adopted mother. She recently asked an aunt in Vallejo for money to pay her room rent but the aunt said she wanted to think about it. When the aunt was contacted later she dismissed the idea of suicide, saying the young woman was always doing something dramatic and threatening to run away. Police, however, said it would have been impossible to walk off the Bridge undetected and listed the event as a suicide. A Security patrol had prevented a man from leaping from almost the exact spot the previous day. The woman's body was never found but the day she is reputed to have jumped...was Leap Year Day.

A socially prominent 24-year-old mother of young twins told her husband she was going to go for a ride one evening in May 1947. She arrived at the Toll Plaza in her late model custom convertible at about 7:30 p.m., handed the toll taker a $5 bill and drove off without waiting for change. The motorist behind her followed to tell her about the change. He was catching up when the woman pulled over and stopped the car, leaving the motor running. As the motorist drove up, the woman ran to the railing and jumped. Her body was not recovered though the Coast Guard searched twice. No suicide note was found, and neither her shocked husband nor father could offer any explanation for her action. A member of a pioneer California family, she was listed as the 81st Bridge suicide.

- - - -

Shortly after midnight on February 17, 1952, patrol officers found a late model car parked just north of the south tower with the motor running and dance music blaring from the radio. A toll taker later told officers he saw someone walk to the railing. Moments earlier a frantic husband had phoned police to tell them he feared his 46-year-old wife might be thinking of jumping off the Bridge. The moving company executive explained to officers later that the couple, who had been married 27 years, "had a family argument, the kind everyone has," earlier that evening. "I don't think we had three arguments in the last two years," he said. "I never thought she would do such a thing. She just loved her grandchildren and brought them presents every time she could."

A daughter said she remembered her mother mentioning

Donner

suicide once before.

"There are so many 'ifs' to this," said the husband. "If I had any idea what she had planned I would have taken the keys to the car or even pulled out one of the wires. She had been despondent because of an illness lately but I thought she had gotten over that."

- - - -

Glenn, a 38-year-old living in Platte, Kansas, received a note from his estranged wife in San Francisco, that said: "Maybe if we could get together we could straighten out our lives. Thanks for your last letter. I cried after I read it. I have missed you. Would it be possible to make a trip out here? You ask about Garry. He went to camp and likes it very much. You're the only person in the world I can turn to. Love and best wishes. Mary."

Glenn made the trip to San Francisco, met with his wife and attempted a reconciliation. She told him, however, that there was no possibility of getting together and that she was planning to marry another man. Glenn left saying he was going to visit a friend in San Rafael, across the Bridge in Marin County. When he walked through the pedestrian gate at the Bridge, he aroused the suspicions of a security officer who started to follow him. As he was running to catch up with the Kansan, Glenn rolled over the railing and fell 185 feet to the concrete surface of the southern anchorage. The wife's note was found in his pocket.

- - - -

When the new bride told her husband she "didn't love him and never had," it proved too much for the young man. He borrowed his father's car and drove to the Bridge, where a passing motorist saw the car stop in mid-span and the driver run across the sidewalk and leap over the east railing. The

Donner

newly-married pair were both 19-years-old.

- - - -

In July 1963, two women jumped to their deaths just 13 days apart to become the 246th and 247th victims. They were both listed as housewives from Novato, a town in Marin County. There was no mention of whether they knew one another or if there was any possible connection.

- - - -

A visitor from Salt Lake City was strolling on the Bridge September 7, 1952, when she saw a woman standing on the railing. "Be careful or you'll fall," she admonished. The woman on the railing replied, "Oh no, I won't fall." The visitor continued walking but when she looked back a few moments later the woman was gone. The visitor looked down and saw the woman's body floating in the moat at the base of the south tower. The husband of the 43-year-old said his wife had been very nervous in recent weeks but had given no hint she planned to end her life.

Another chat ended in the same fashion after a woman, walking on the Bridge around 4 p.m. on May 1, 1968, saw a well-dressed woman in her 30's standing on the other side of the railing. "Although it was apparent, I asked her what she was doing. She looked at me kind of strangely and said, 'Now, you take my coat and my purse, there's a lot of money in it.' Then just as the rescue trucks were arriving she jumped," said the witness. The Daly City woman died 15 minutes after hitting the water and was pronounced dead on arrival at the hospital. Separated from her husband, she was the 342nd known suicide. Officers found $73 in her purse.

- - - -

The note, scribbled in green ink, simply said, "Loved ones: My nerves are all shot. Pleae forgive me." The note was found in a blue serge coat tied to a Bridge painter's tool box, and supposedly belonged to a newly-elected San Francisco Supervisor. His secretary said he left the jewelry store where he was an executive, at 5 p.m. and in seemingly good spirits. He went to pick up his car but was told the service on it had not been completed. No one saw him jump or walk out on the Bridge and no body was recovered. Neither his wife nor business associates could explain the apparent suicide. It was rumored in City Hall, however, he had been the subject of political black mail and that he was exhaused from a grueling election campaign.

- - - -

A 32-year-old woman took a bus from El Monte, California, to The City, checked her luggage in a terminal locker and took a cab to the Bridge, arriving around 6 p.m. She approached a Bridge attendant and asked him if he would hold her purse while she went to get something to eat at the Roundhouse restaurant. The attendant was busy and didn't notice that the woman by-passed the restaurant and started walking toward the span. When she reached the south tower, she slipped over the side. At that very second, another visitor was at Vista Point on the north end watching her fall through binoculars. He immediately notified authorities, who retrieved her body from the concrete tower base. In her note she left a flashlight and $8 in her purse to the Bridge attendant.

- - - -

The 254th known suicide from the Bridge spent five years working in the coroner's office transcribing notes on autopsies of suicides. The 42-year-old San Franciscan, left his coat and wallet but no note in the car he parked on the span. The coroner's office said the man had been getting psychiatric counseling.

Donner

- - - -

On February 12, 1971, another strange event occurred which is rare in the annals of Bridge suicide accounts. A witness saw a 24-year-old San Francisco woman take off a sweater, place her purse on the walkway, climb over the railing on the east side near the north tower and jump. As the Coast Guard sped to the scene to search for the body, they were hailed by a passing boat whose crew said they saw the body and that a shark was attacking it. The Coast Guard had to drive the shark away with boathooks before they could recover the body. Huge chunks of flesh had been torn away from one thigh. Crew members believed the woman was killed on impact.

"Sometimes the sharks and other marine life get the body," recounted another Coast Guardsman. "I picked up one woman who floated up toward Alcatraz and her flesh had pretty well been cleaned off by sharks and other marine life," he said. (*See Chapter Eleven*).

- - - -

In October of the same year the 427th suicide victim, a 22-year-old student from a university in Oregon, leaped from center-span on the east side. Witnesses saw him doffing his jacket and shoes and putting something in his mouth before mounting the rail. When the Coast Guard recovered his body, they found $36 in bills in his mouth.

- - - -

A Harbor Queen cruise ship from Fisherman's Wharf with 125 tourists aboard was just turning back into the Bay and passing beneath the Bridge at approximately 10:20 a.m. on October 4, 1976. At the Toll Plaza a sergeant was monitoring the road television surveillance camera when he saw a woman acting peculiarly near center-span. A nearby painter also thought she was acting strangely and started running toward her, but she squeezed through a separation in the railing when the painter was barely 15 feet away and jumped.

Horrified tourists aboard the vessel watched her body fall horizontally during the 260-foot plunge. The captain saw a "tremendous splash" not 50 yards ahead, and within seconds the woman was visible on the surface. Two deckhands, dangling from a passenger entryway, were able to pull her aboard as the captain called for medical help on the public address system. One physician and one dentist responded, administering heart massage and mouth-to-mouth resuscitation.

"The young woman hit the water so close to the boat," said the dentist, "I thought for a slecond she was going to hit the bow."

As the Harbor Queen tied up at the Wharf, passengers were stunned and most refused to talk about the incident.

However, one commented, "She was a beautiful young girl. If this were an old man we would not have been so emotionally affected."

A CHP patrol car took the woman to Letterman Hospital, where she died an hour and 40 minutes later during exploratory surgery.

The 33-year-old resident of Sausalito had jumped with a cardboard box containing the cremated remains of a former female roommate, said police.

- - - -

Another spectacular ringside seat to a suicide came one morning as the traffic helicopter of a local TV station was hovering near the north tower reporting on the Marin commute. A motorist saw a woman climb the rail near the north tower and told officers at the Toll Plaza. A bulletin was put out over the Security band which was picked up by the helicopter pilot. Both he and the traffic reporter watched the 29-year-

old woman from Santa Rosa fall feet first to the Bay.
"She plummeted down just like a rocket," said the pilot. "When she hit the water we really were shocked and stunned. A geyser shot into the air at least 20 feet high. When she surfaced she was floating on her stomach with head and feet down. The impact had torn the clothes off her back."

- - - -

The eldest son of a former famous White House staffer died from a leap in February 1977. A Bridge painter saw the victim climb over the east railing near the south tower and run about 50 feet on the catwalk chord before leaping. The body was recovered by the Coast Guard and identified by papers in his wallet and by his grief-stricken mother. The 28-year-old New York University graduate had returned recently to San Francisco and was looking for a job.

- - - -

A fishing boat spotted the body of a man floating near the Bridge on the morning of May 26, 1977, and pulled alongside to retrieve it. The body was floating face down and when the crew pulled it aboard, they found a five-inch hunting knife protruding from the man's chest.

- - - -

At 10 a.m. on August 18, 1973, church bells throughout the Bay Area began a mournful tolling to commemorate the 491 known victims who jumped from the Bridge. The ceremony was carefully planned and executed but had communications been better or faster, the bells would have tolled not 491, but 492.

Less than two hours before the bells began pealing, a Bridge security captain pulled over near the north tower where he noticed a young man standing glumly at the railing.

Asked what he was doing, the young man replied he was a photographer studying the surroundings for a later photo session. He said he left his camera gear in his van parked at Vista Point.

A CHP patrol car with two officers pulled up just then and joined in the questioning asking to see the man's photo equipment. As the officers were escorting him to the patrol car, the man bolted to the railing and "cartwheeled" over the barrier landing on the rocks of Lime Point. The 27-year-old was the son of the scion of one of this country's oldest and most distinguished families. He was the second eldest of eight children and a 1969 Princeton graduate. His father, who identified the body over the phone from a description of surgical scars, said his son sent him a letter a week ago waxing "optimistically and enthusiastically about his future."

- - - -

A cyclist rode onto the Bridge in early May 1975, and casually parked his bike near the south tower. Then he crawled over the railing to the two-and-a-half-foot wide girder below and sat there. Two CHP officers arrived within minutes and tried to talk the man back up, but as they watched helplessly the man shoved himself from the girder and fell. The Coast Guard recovered his body a mile out to sea.

- - - -

Angie was young--she would be 33 in three weeks-- an attractive, tall brunette with blue eyes, and multi-talented as an accomplished cellist, sailing instructor and former high school teacher. She was also described by friends and co-workers as "a woman who didn't realize how gifted she was. As well as she did, she couldn't please herself," said one.

Donner

    Her brother stated his sister had been "a very idealistic person but after her marriage several years ago didn't work out, she lost a great deal of that idealism." He added that a "skiing accident also may have led to her collapse. She ran into a tree and it was very quick after that."

    Although she had "an awful lot of friends and everyone liked her, she was sensitive and vulnerable to the alienation from being a single woman," said another friend.

    Born in Berkeley, Angie went to Stanford where she was an honor student in humanities and then earned a teaching credential at the University of California in Berkeley.

    She had been under a psychologist's care for several years and had once been escorted from the Bridge because she was acting strangely. On July 9, 1980, she paid another visit to the Bridge and at 2:30 p.m. ended her short life.

    Asked if he knew why his sister committed suicide, the brother replied, "No, I didn't have the chance to ask her."

- - - -

    One person said the 38-year-old was a brilliant actress in Germany before she came to the States. Others said she suffered terrible bouts of depression and would simply "drop out" for long periods. One account told of how she met her architect husband when he photographed her with the Bridge as a backdrop, an eerie prediction of things to come, because on September 17, 1981, she leaped to her death off the Bridge.

    Although her body was recovered by the Coast Guard within a few minutes, there was no clue as to her identity.

    "We tried everything," said the San Francisco coroner's office. "She was obviously a very attractive woman, well groomed and well clothed, but nothing worked. We sent around teeth charts, fingerprints but nothing turned up."

After routine checks her file was buried in the staggering number of missing persons reports which average about 3,000 a year in The City. In December the staff of the Missing Persons Unit was doubled, and an officer was assigned to recheck delicate cases. The woman's husband had filed a missing person's report, stating that it was not unusual for his wife to be absent for months during their ten years of marriage. He said when she was ready to return, she would call him and he would get her.

The agent checking through the backlog found a match in the coroner's office and called the husband to see if he could identify her. He did, four months after the body was recovered from the Bay.

- - - -

For several days the identity of the barefoot man dressed in white dress shirt and black slacks, who hurled himself off the Bridge in October 1994, remained unknown. The Marin county coroner described the victim as well-dressed and well kept, "he will be missed by someone."

When investigators discovered an abandoned car near the Bridge with a suicide note, the man's identity was revealed but why he ended his life remained a deep mystery. The family did not disclose the contents of the note.

The father of four children, he was a brilliant 46-year-old attorney and accountant, whose expertise in international bank and corporate tax issues took him around the world.

"It was the biggest shock of my life and I have been around death a lot," said a colleague. "He really had this transcendency of soul. There are very few people like that in this world. As an attorney he never banged on the table, he commanded respect through his knowledge."

Friends described him as a good-natured, self-possessed

person who didn't seem the type to be stressed out in any way. "This is very difficult to understand and accept. I don't think there is anyone I've talked to who had seen any hint of trouble," said a close friend. "I got a letter from him yesterday saying he was looking forward to working with me for a mutual client."

The victim was the sixth leaper within two weeks. When a reporter called for more details about the "barefoot leaper," a Bridge officer said hastily, "I can't talk to you now, we have a woman hanging over the edge." The woman was perched on the east railing threatening to jump, but officers were able to grab her before she made good on her threat.

- - -

A 19-year-old college student from Virginia--just one week shy of his 20th birthday--was described as "very popular and seemed to distinguish himself at everything he did," including his final act of becoming the 987th confirmed suicide from the Bridge.

On Saturday, March 18, 1995, he slipped on his backpack, left his college dorm in Williamsburg, Virginia., and, without telling anyone where he was going or how long he would be gone, cycled to the student union then "disappeared" from the College of William & Mary campus. He left family and friends wondering specifically how he got to San Francisco, how he paid for the airline ticket, why he chose The City and, most importantly, why, at 11:15 that same night he hurled himself from mid-span on the east side.

A champion swimmer who had participated in the sport since he was seven, he set two state records in high school and was captain of the team. He continued swimming in college but suddenly quit the team six months previously. His coach suggested the lad "might have felt a void in his life since it was the first time he didn't have that kind of an outlet. I don't think any of us here can really understand why this happened. There was nothing. There was no letter. We're in the dark..."

His grieving family expressed hopes that someone in San Francisco would be able to shed light on the tragedy.

As the official number of leapers moved inexorably toward the 1,000 figure, Bridge authorities were bracing for a rash of attempts despite an apparent news blackout.

Chapter Ten:

The Grim Statistics

An average of one person every three weeks has jumped from the Bridge. The average leapers per year is 17. Those are statistical averages, but it obviously doesn't happen that way. There have been four suicides within a 24-hour period, and months when no one used the Bridge for a final exit.

Bridge "watchers" and some psychologists offer what might be called an "epidemic theory," in which one suicide sparks a rash of them. Researchers also say there is no correlation between the number of suicides and the time of year except around the holidays when the deaths are more common. Several have jumped on Christmas Eve and Christmas Day and the numbers increase during the fourth quarter of the year. There are more intense times than others and people react accordingly, said Peter Sibbson, a spokesman for the Suicide Prevention Agency and Crisis Hotline.

The Bridge had its first official suicide nine weeks after it opened May 27, 1937. There were five official leapers the first year; six the following year, and only three in 1939. For some reason, (the war?) the number jumped to 15 in 1940.

The "100th jumper", a 31-year-old San Francisco woman, was recorded by San Francisco newspapers on June 28, 1948. She was identified by papers in a purse left near the span's north tower. A note to her husband found in the purse, said she was "sorry...but no soap. I'm leaving now and hope you're happy."

The husband told police his wife was "tempestuous, nervous and had threatened suicide in the past." He said both were motorcycle enthusiasts and that he asked his wife to accompany him to Santa Cruz for a cycle meet but she refused and went to Marin to watch a similar contest. The husband said he suspected his wife might have planted the purse to "throw a scare" into him. No one witnessed the jump nor was any body found.

Bridge authorities also suspected a hoax and didn't list the woman as an official suicide.

The official 100th suicide, recorded later the same day, was a visitor from Mexico City. All that is known is that he stopped two boys walking on the Bridge and said, "I am from Mexico City, give me a cigarette." They gave him one and walked away. They turned back and saw him take off his coat, mount the rail and plunge to his death.

As of this date. 1948, 74 men and 26 women had jumped to their deaths.

The 200th victim, a 32-year-old woman from San Francisco, was logged 12 years later on December 30, 1960. It was about 1:40 p.m. when two boys reported seeing a blond-haired woman, wearing glasses and a tan coat, walk to the south tower. The two teens, who were on vacation from school, saw the woman stop at the rail and gaze toward The City and Alcatraz. They thought she was just taking in the spectacular view, but then she took off her coat and dropped it, along with her purse, to the walkway. She turned her back to the railing, boosted herself up and sat there for a moment. Then she kicked off her shoes and did a backward somersault over the rail. The Coast Guard was unable to recover the body.

The 300th official suicide from the Bridge came six years later on April 11, 1966. The victim, a young man who worked in The City, was followed in death the next day by his close friend. There were 16 official leapers in that year whereas 1967 and 1968 saw a total of 42 suicides from the Bridge.

It took only four years before the 400th suicide was recorded in October 1970 and only three years to reach number 500 on October 10, 1973.

"He was a kind, generous and talented young man," said the brother of the 500th victim, "and when you were with him he seemed happy and gentle. But he just couldn't cope with what was happening around him. It wasn't political or social, it was personal."

The 26-year-old blood technician at a San Francisco hospital was estranged from his wife, who worked at a hospital in Monterey. He lived in a Haight street commune with a group of friends, one of whom told police he saw the young man around 4:30 p.m., and that he seemed in good spirits. Two hours later, however, his body was on the rocks below the north tower on the east side of the Bridge.

Police found a yellow pickup truck parked at Vista Point with a reminder notebook inside that had a message scrawled over two pages saying the truck belonged to his brother, and asking that his mother, "who has a heart problem, not be notified." The complete contents of the note were not disclosed but a coroner's deputy reported "it said he wasn't sad or mad at anybody, but that he just felt this was the thing to do."

The victim's brother said he didn't have any feelings about the Bridge. "Frankly, I think my brother would have found a place whether or not there was a barrier on the Bridge," he said.

Less than 24 hours later a 48-year-old housewife from Corte Madera, became number 501.

Parents of the 600th leaper were on their way from Kelseyville in Lake County in Northern Californa to visit their daughter but had car trouble near Santa Rosa. They spent the night with a friend nearby and tried to phone their daughter but were unable to reach her. The reason was that the 24-year-old unemployed medical lab technician was lying in the moat surrounding the south tower of the Bridge. She had leaped at 5:25 p.m. on May 28, 1977, one day after the 40th anniversary of the opening of the span.

The father described his daughter as "a kind of loner," with few friends. She lived by herself in The City and had not worked for two years because of a disability. She had attempted suicide twice within the past three months, according to her father.

A memorial service for the 600 victims was held the next day near the Strauss statue at the south entrance of the Bridge. Participants wore black arm bands and carried the names of those who died, 24 of which occurred that year.

On October 8, 1981, a Marin youth became number 700 and on February 21, 1984, a 66-year-old Golden Gate Bridge engineer used the span to end his life. The 900th death occurred on June 24, 1991 and the "official" 1,000th....?

Chapter Eleven:

The Rescuers

The call came in to the Bridge Security office that a woman had gone over the railing near the south tower. Ron Garcia and another lieutenant sped to the scene and were joined by a tow-truck operator and a CHP officer. The woman, about 40 years old, was sitting on the chord, the two-and-a-half-foot wide girder that forms a catwalk on the other side of the railing.

"Usually when someone is out there long enough to get to them, you can stop them because they have doubts in their mind if they wait that long," said Garcia. "But this woman seemed determined to do it. As we were talking to her she starts slipping off the chord, just sliding herself off.

"The other lieutenant and I had already put on our safety equipment (a harness-like device that hooks onto ironwork) and I went over the rail," said Garcia. "Just as I got on the other side, she gave herself another shove, but I was able to grab her arm just as she went over. I was pulled flat on my chest against the chord but hung on as she dangled above the water. You can't really do any lifting when you're flat against that girder, so we had a heck of a time getting her back onto the chord."

Garcia hung on for what seemed like an eternity while the other lieutenant and the tow-truck driver scrambled over the rail to help pull the leaper to safety.

"The problem with this particular case," Garcia said,

"was that this person was a walk-away from a psychiatric ward and they knew she was suicidal. They notified our office a half hour after we got her off the Bridge. If we had known ahead of time maybe we could have stopped her before she got to the point she did.

"Was it scary? Well, you don't think of it at the time. You're too busy," said Garcia, who is now Captain of the Bridge Emergency Service Force. In August 1995, he marked 27 years with the Bridge. His predecessor, Capt. Jackson Fong, who retired in January 1995, had more than 34 years with the force.

- - - -

California Highway Patrolman John Allison was driving toward the Marin side of the Bridge at 8 p.m. one evening when he saw a tall figure climb over the rail and leap. He radioed the Coast Guard to come to mid-span on the east side then got out to take a look. He was astonished to see a man in his early 20's on the chord on the other side of the railing.

"Why don't you go away," yelled the youth, "I don't want to get in any trouble."

"If I go away will you come up?" Allison shouted.

At this point the youth had climbed down to a scaffold used by Bridge painters and was dangling by his fingers.

"OK, I'll go away, but you come up," said the patrolman who had several "saves" to his credit.

The youth managed to get back on the scaffold, then onto the chord from where he crawled back over the railing to safety. Trembling with his flirtation with death, he refused to explain his actions to Allison, though he did admit to vaulting over the Bridge entrance railing, by-passing the pedestrian toll gate which costs a dime.

"Some people are just waiting to be stopped," said Garcia. "We actually do stop others from jumping. Some are looking for attention or someone to talk to. If you count everyone each one of us took off the Bridge and counseled over the years, eighty does not seem like a large number."

The Emergency Service Force, consisting of 16 people usually working four to a shift, keeps a log but their figures and those of the CHP do not correspond. They basically use the CHP tally of leapers as the official one, said Garcia, who recalled one year in the late 1970's as being the "biggest year" for suicides with more than 40 recorded.

The CHP is the official agency for traffic control while the Bridge force handles some security, accident investigation, suicide prevention and toll collection. Both respond to someone's threatening to jump. Bridge Security also handles the television surveillance which monitors traffic as well as "people acting suspiciously."

"This is something you learn on the job," said Garcia about spotting potential suicides. "You can pass along all sorts of tips and suggestions of what to look for, but you just have to develop a sixth sense about those who are contemplating suicide."

The District provides special training for its Security Force regarding suicide prevention as well as personal counseling to staff when there is such a need.

"But I've never had anyone come to the point where they needed time off the Bridge because of mental or psychological stress," said Garcia. "However, I think the suicides affect everybody. The main thing we have to do is figure that we did everything we could. You might second-guess yourself and think, 'What if I had done this or that?' but it's pointless because you could do that forever, then all of a sudden feel real guilty and that doesn't do anybody any good."

Predicting suicides, despite graphs and charts, is near impossible. Security officers will tell you to expect at least one attempt per week, but there are the other times, like September 18, 1963, where the would-be suicide action was so brisk the officers hardly had time to get a cup of coffee.

Shortly after 1 a.m. that day motorists reported a man in his shirtsleeves walking toward the Bridge through the Funston tunnel. Officers picked up the 35-year-old grocery store operator and as their car slowed near the Toll Plaza, the man jumped out and ran toward the railing. The officers wrestled the man to the ground and handcuffed him.

Four hours later a 33-year-old man from Redwood City drove to Vista Point where he scribbled a note to his daughter: "Daddy loves you more than he can bear. Love -- sorry. Daddy." Officers spotted him walking toward the center of the span looking confused, and when approached, he told them he was having family problems.

Fifteen minutes later, two soldiers were driving south across the Bridge headed to the Presidio when they came upon a car parked in the middle of the span, and saw a 21-year-old Oakland man standing at the railing. They persuaded him to accompany them to the Bridge Security office where he told weary officers he was having "girlfriend trouble."

Some bridgeworkers have volunteered to assist in saving would-be leapers and their help is welcomed as they deal with heights every day climbing all over the span. On call 24 hours a day, they have been credited with saving numerous lives, as have other workers who phoned for rescuers when their "sixth sense" was aroused.

Donner

"We have the rigging and we don't have to stop and think, 'What are we stepping on' or 'What's in the way?'" said a veteran ironworker.

Others involved in rescue work are the valiant and seldom-hailed men and women of the U.S. Coast Guard.

One who went above and beyond the line of duty--and to this day is still wondering "what on earth possessed me to do it"--is Senior Chief Boson's Mate Ron Wilton. Stationed at Fort Point in 1986, he left one afternoon and was returning to his home in Novato, across the Bridge in Marin County, when he saw a tow truck and patrol car stopped on the northbound lane at mid-span with emergency lights flashing.

"I thought at first it was a stalled car but as I got closer I saw a female sheriff's deputy leaning over the rail trying to help somebody and holding pedestrians back with hand signals," he recalled. "I pulled over in front of the patrol car and approached her identifying myself.

"I asked her if she needed help and when I looked over the rail I saw two male deputies lying on the catwalk, one had a line tied around his waist with a couple of turns tied around a stanchion. The other deputy was just lying on the catwalk, hanging onto the railing with one hand. What they had in their other hands was the clothing of a woman who was dangling above the water," he said.

The woman had gone over the rail as a "hanger" and was sitting on the chord when the deputies arrived. They had gotten a grasp on her, but she had wriggled free and at this point was hanging onto the railing. One deputy had lowered himself over the side with a safety line tied on. The woman, in her late 30's, was struggling with him when the second deputy went over the side without a safety line to help his partner. The two were trying to pull the woman back up onto the girder when Wilton arrived.

"When I looked over and saw what was happening with the two deputies, and saw the woman's sweater sort of ripping away from them as they tried to hang on to her, I don't know what possessed me, but I leaped over the rail and partially landed on top one of the deputies. I reached down and grabbed the back of the woman's jeans and got a strong hold, which allowed the deputies to grab her under each armpit. Together we just sort of hurled her up over the railing where the female deputy wrestled her to the ground," Wilton recalled.

"I climbed back over the rail myself and tried to stop my legs from trembling. I looked over the rail and saw the two deputies, who were completely exhausted at this point. It took the female deputy and me at least ten minutes to get them back up and onto the sidewalk, where the three of us just sort of sat there for a minute, shaking our heads as though asking 'What are we doing?' Like I said, to this day I don't know what on earth possessed me, but I just saw a need, and that something had to be done," said the Chief.

Wilton spent four years at the Fort Point station from 1984 to 1987. The crews work shifts something like firemen, 48 hours on, and 48 hours off. The territorial range for the Fort Point crews is from Pier 39 to Alcatraz and Angel Island west up to and beyond the Bridge. Retrieving the bodies of leapers has taken them all the way to Land's End at the shoreline of the Pacific Ocean. Crews have to estimate the state of the tide to plot where bodies may have drifted, presuming they stayed afloat. In a maximum ebbtide most bodies are never recovered because of the strong undertow that drags the victims out to sea. When possible, Bridge officers will drop smoke flares that float for up to 45

Donner

45 minutes, guiding crews toward the site where the body landed.

"As a rule, if it's an out-going tide, we'll search as far as Land's End and out into the main bar channel," Wilton said. "Most searches pretty well terminate when you start to head off-shore, but we did recover one body just past Land's End, a heavy-set man, who drifted straight off-shore."

In his second year at Fort Point Wilton was involved in retrieving one of the 19 known survivors. The call came in at 8:15 a.m. that someone had jumped from center span on the east side.

"It just so happened we were at a slack tide, a time when the water is almost flat calm," Wilton recalled. "There were no wind-generated waves and no current. I proceeded out with a crew on a 30-foot surf rescue boat, which is very fast. As we approached the center of the Bridge we saw something moving around in the water. At first I thought it was a seal, possibly playing with the floater. I told the crew to keep an eye on it. As we got closer we could see it was a man swimming toward us. He must have entered the water feet first, and because there was no current to suck him under and it was calm, he survived the jump. When we came alongside I asked him, 'Did you just jump from the Bridge?' and he said, 'Yes, I did.' He was conscious of what he had done, and seemed in good shape despite a couple of broken ribs, punctured lung and minor lacerations. He was released from the hospital three days later."

Sometimes the Coast Guard will be summoned for a "hanger," a person who has gone over the rail and is threatening to jump, but hasn't made the final move.

"We've responded to these situations," Wilton said, "and just sat underneath the person waiting to see what was going to happen. One time someone did jump and we recovered the body. On two other occasions they were apprehended by sheriff's deputies."

During his four years at Fort Point Wilton was involved in retrieving numerous jumpers and, as would be expected, some were in bad shape with heads twisted backward, bones protruding or part of the body split open from the impact. He recalled one of his worst, a 22-year-old woman who jumped from the south tower on the east side.

"She didn't project far enough from the railing when she pushed off and landed face first on the exterior of the cement fender surrounding the moat. Her face was pretty well shaved off from the back of her chin to the front. There was no real face there," he said.

"It's usually not so much what happens to jumpers externally but internally," said the Chief. "It's like someone took an eggbeater to the organs of the body and ground everything up because of the compression impact."

A Coast Guard boat and crew stand ready for rescue work around the clock, 365 days a year, and some days can be harrowing. Wilton recalled one during the summer of 1986 when the Bay was crowded with boaters.

"We had Search and Rescue (SAR) calls all day. The station's resources had been underway almost all day responding to different calls, vessels needing a tow, vessels going on the rocks, people in the water etc. We just had a very busy day with a lot of cases taking place. Towards mid-afternoon, among all these SAR cases going on, we had a call for a jumper. We had one vessel that was already engaged in a SAR operation, another one proceeding to an operation and one vessel tied to the dock.

"We got the third vessel underway to respond to this

Donner

jumper. They no sooner got back from retrieving the body when they got call to a SAR themselves. This was going on all day long. Somewhere around five p.m. one of the boats was on its way in from a case when we got a call for another jumper. So they diverted from returning to the station, located and recovered the body and called the coroner's office.

"They were cleaning up their vessel as the second vessel returned to the station and started cleaning up. It was now about six p.m. and the third vessel was just returning from its SAR case and getting moored up. The crews were walking down the dock when the alarm went off again, and then the announcement over the loudspeaker, 'Jumper, center span,' the third of the day. I remember looking out my office window and seeing the crews dashing back to their boats when they heard the first alarm, then slow to a trot when they heard the announcement of the jumper. I could see it was wearing on them at this point.

"They recovered that third body," he continued, "and when all the boats were in and secured, we got a call from the coroner's office to let us know that the two previous jumpers both had tested positive for Hepatitis B and one for AIDS as well. They were passing that information on to us as standard procedure, because at the time, there was a lot unknown about the AIDS virus. When that information came in at the end of this exhausting day, it was the final straw. It put the entire unit into a tailspin trying to cope with it all. What was stressing the crew the most was that they were willing to go as long and as hard as it took to save lives, and they realized that was their duty and their job. But it was this having to recover those who took their own lives mixed in with their work to save lives that wore on them pretty heavy that day.

Donner

"Nobody in their right mind wants to do this sort of thing forever," said Wilton, currently assigned to the Motor Life Boat Station at Bodega Bay in northern California. "But there are so many other good things about duty at the station to make up for having to deal with that. It just comes with the territory."

In late 1989, the Coast Guard station moved from Fort Point on the San Francisco side to Fort Baker on the Marin shore. It was a move long in coming since, for years, there were discussions about how "near impossible" it was to maintain the vessels in proper condition at Fort Point, how there was no protection for the boats while moored, how difficult it was to tie up boats because of the waves and strong current. When it became apparent there would be no improvements or up-grading at the Fort Point site, the station moved across the channel into Horseshoe cove at Fort Baker. It was the most logical option because of its enclosed harbor and the nearness to the Bridge. During World War II a Coast Guard unit had been assigned there along with military units who manned the picket boats that guarded the Bay.

The current commanding officer of the Coast Guard unit at Fort Baker is Chief Warrant Officer William J. Lee, who took over March 6, 1995. There were five jumpers his first month. The unit has a 44-foot cutter moored there which requires a minimum crew of four to operate. When we interviewed him in early May, 1995, there had been a leaper just the day before (but no story appeared in the papers).

"As soon as we get notification from whatever source, the crew gets underway within two minutes," said Lee. "Yesterday's call came from an operator of one of the Red and White Fleet tourist ferryboats. It stood by in the vicinity until we arrived to recover the body, which we did in less than 12 minutes. We also go out when there's a possible jumper as well."

Lee, who has been involved in rescue work here and in the Great Lakes region, said, "If we don't get them right away we end up getting them later and it's a lot worse. The bodies are badly decomposed with what the coroner's reports describe as 'evidence of severe marine depredation,' meaning nearly picked clean, mostly from crabs. You may think twice, now, before you have that next crab sandwich. Anytime the crew has to witness something like that, it's not pleasant."

Chief Lee said that when staff are assigned to the station they typically have no special training in this type of work, so the unit provides it for the staff of 30, including psychological counseling.

"One crew member was involved in recovering the body of a kid whose dad threw the child over the railing. (See Chapter Six). It was very shocking, and he consequently had to have therapy to keep it together," said Lee.

"We don't know from the second we get underway whether we'll lay eyes on the victim, so we don't notify the emergency medical system until the boat crew reports they have the victim in sight. We continue the search until we're told to stand down, which comes from the controllers who work for the District Commander, the admiral on Alameda.

"We work closely with the Bridge Authority," he continued. "They get a lot of business on the south tower because they have to fish out the victims who land in the moat and then turn the bodies over to us. They help us tremendously in getting to the victims," said Chief Lee.

When we asked Capt. Martin Nemiroff, M.D., why some bodies sink and others do not, he said there were a lot of factors and pulled up his multi-faceted answer on his computer screen. Nemiroff, Division Chief of Health Services with the U.S. Coast Guard Support Center on Alameda, said he gets asked this question all over the country.

"Age is a factor," he started in. "The younger they are, the better they float because of body fat and mass. Fat tends to float. A body can float from minutes, to hours, to days to never. Sex is another variable. Females tend to float more readily because of more body fat. There are also racial differences. Black races in general are not good floaters. Body weight is important, the more weight, the more fat and consequently the more float. What people are wearing is a factor if there is air entrapped in what they're wearing. Some people think shoes drag you down, but it's just the opposite. Shoes trap air and make you more floatable. Other determinants are the recency of a meal, since more air is trapped in some types of food, or if you drink a soda, it would create more gas in the body and tend to provide more flotation.

"Water temperature is another determinant," he continued. "Well-known cold bodies of water, like Lake Tahoe or Lake Superior, never give up their bodies. There tends to be less flotation in colder water. Salt water is more buoyant that fresh water. The state of the sea is important, whether it's calm or whether there's a lot of wave action.
The weather is a definite determinant. And the depth of the water. Significant portions under the Golden Gate Bridge are 40-feet deep and we've actually had people who have rebounded off the bottom and came back to surface.

"Injuries can change the flotation of a body, such as letting entrapped air out," Captain Nemiroff explained. "Any animal or fish entry into the body can change the flotation characteristics. Fish enter various orifices of the body and eat away part of the body and that will affect the flotation factors. The longer the body is in the water and floating, the longer it will stay up because postmortem gas develops and aids flotation."

Asked about hypothermia, the physician said the Bay is cold most of the time with temperatures in the high 40's and low 50's.

"We generally measure survival in *useful conscious time*, and if there is no trauma, useful conscious time for people in the water could be twenty minutes. But many jumpers are dead on impact so there is no useful conscious time. If they become unconscious they don't have a clear airway to breathe so they take in water and drown. Once you lose consciousness in the water you generally don't remain afloat.

"I'm giving you general parameters of survival but it could go from minutes to days. There are people who have survived in that water for long periods. There is something that is immeasurable called the will to live. There are some who have a tremendous desire to stay alive and exceed everything we do with paper and pencil. There are others who do not want to live so they don't last very long," he said.

The physician said Coast Guard people are taught various survival techniques, such as what to think about, telling jokes, thinking of one's family. He recalled the case of a woman who was shipwrecked on an island in Alaska for three weeks and kept herself alive by thinking of what toppings she was going to order on her pizza.

Captain Nemiroff was also engaged in research concerning the response time of Coast Guard rescue crews and recounted a time when one crew in the unit's rigid-hull inflatable was on a training mission under the Bridge when a leaper landed 15

Donner

feet in front of them.

"It was nearly a direct hit," he chortled. "Our response time was zero, and you can't improve on that."

Chapter Twelve:

The Battle Over the Barriers

A 38-year-old San Francisco engineer was walking near mid-span on the east side carrying a sign that read: "Please support a suicide barrier." At the same time, 10:25 a.m., on May 9, 1978, a 44-year-old woman, who had recently come to The City and was jobless, climbed the railing just beyond the south tower and plunged to her death. The demonstrator was unaware the Bridge had claimed its 639th victim.

The engineer was warned by CHP officers that his demonstration was illegal and if he continued he would be arrested, fined or sent to prison. The Golden Gate Bridge District does not allow demonstrations on the span because drivers might become distracted and cause accidents. The demonstrator explained that he wanted to keep the issue of a suicide barrier before the public because he had "concern for people."

Discussions on how to prevent suicides from the Bridge started as early as February 1939. As a police craft searched for the body of a 50-year-old former secretary of the San Jose Chamber of Commerce, Bridge authorities pondered the problem of prevention. The man, estranged from his wife, was the 11th recorded jumper. Officers stated they had talked the man out of jumping several weeks earlier. Only two years old, "the Bridge was becoming a Mecca for despondent people," one newspaper editorialized.

Donner

In the 1960's closed-circuit television cameras were installed over the roadway on the bottom strut of both towers, as well as on the Toll Plaza and administration building. The cameras swing 360 degrees and can zoom in to pick up an individual along the railing. They were installed originally for traffic monitoring but are used heavily today for people surveillance on a 24-hour basis. A second set of cameras designed for low-level night viewing has also been installed.

There are a total of 13 emergency phones located on the Bridge with the capability of being patched into the San Francisco Suicide Prevention hotline. In addition, employees receive special training on suicide prevention, and several bridgeworkers make themselves available around the clock to assist in rescues.

Through the years there have been calls for suicide barriers on the Bridge. Ironically, an early proponent of a suicide barrier was the Rev. Jim Jones, who later led 912 of his followers from San Francisco to commit suicide in the jungles of Guyana.

At a special Bridge seminar in 1968, one suicide expert testified that a barrier would cause The City to loose its rapidly-growing reputation as a Mecca for suicides. He was rebutted, however, by the state health director who felt a barrier would have no effect on the suicide rate since those bent on taking their lives would find another way.

In June 1973 there was another hearing regarding suicide barriers and a report heard from Richard J. Seiden, Ph.D., Director of the Golden Gate Bridge Study at the University of California at Berkeley. His statementsaid in part:

"It is important to note that this problem of suicide epidemics is a long standing one. Sometimes the spot at which a person had chosen to kill himself exercised a weird fascination on others, then setting up a wave of suicides on that spot.

"In France, at the Invalides, there were no suicides for two years when a soldier hung himself from a beam in one corridor. Within a short time 12 others had followed his example, stringing themselves up to the same beam," (quoted from H.R. Feden *Suicide: A Social and Historical Study*, 1938).

Seiden stated further that "Less than four percent of Golden Gate Bridge suicide attempters have gone on to commit suicide. Surveys recommended putting up a barrier. It is too tempting to people who are distressed or disturbed. One victim who died in a leap left this poignant question in a suicide note: 'Why do you make it so easy?'"

Another document developed by the School of Public Health at the University of California, Berkeley, stated: "The Golden Gate Bridge is well known as one of the world's most beautiful bridges but it also has the unhappy reputation of being a suicide landmark of epidemic proportions...This slender strand has been the termination point for hundreds of human lives. Just how many, will probably never be known, but of one thing we can be certain, the report of the number of suicide deaths, which is now approaching 500, is an overly conservative figure which substantially underestimates the actual dimensions of the problem. The true magnitude of suicide deaths is considerably greater. If an effective suicide prevention program using a barrier is to be developed, two basic questions must be considered: a) why do certain locations obtain suicide reputations, and b) will preventing suicide deaths at a particular location simply transfer suicides to another site.

The argument that suicides will go some place else does not bear up under objective examination and experience of other suicide landmarks nor in studies dealing with suicide patients."

There have been 18 suicide barrier proposals including a) a 9-foot barbed wire fence, 2) U-shaped spikes, 3) Nylon safety net on both sides, 4) Plexiglas screen on top of rail, 5) laser beam, 6) chain link fence, and 7) a rotating horizontal cylinder on top of the railing.

Among the criteria a barrier must meet are: a) it cannot be a hazard to pedestrians or maintenance crews, b) it must be totally effective, c) its weight cannot exceed 144 pounds per linear foot.

The District spent $27,000 investigating one design, an 8-foot high railing, but tests showed the thin rods could be easily bent.

When the business of erecting a suicide barrier came up for vote in 1973, Bridge District supervisors were against it, claiming insufficient funds.

"We should forget it (a barrier) till it's financially feasible, much as I hate to say that," said one.

"If it can be shown to me it can save a life, even if it costs $2 million, I'm for it," said another, who also voted against it.

Bridge authorities concluded that because a barrier would also be an eyesore it would not be "acceptable to the public."

In 1974 the cost of putting up a barrier was estimated at $2.7 million. The latest 1995 estimate was $6.9 million.

A poll in 1977 on a proposed barrier revealed Bay Area residents were evenly split on the issue.

That same year the parents of a 19-year-old boy, who leaped from the span, filed a $1 million lawsuit against Bridge officials, accusing them of "negligently and carelessly" failing to provide barriers.

Another lawsuit was filed against the Bridge District in 1994, charging officials with failing to do enough to prevent leaps from the span. The suit was filed by a mother, running for a political office, who didn't find out about her 32-year-old son's death until three weeks later. Witnesses on the Bridge and in a sailboat reported the leap. The man left his wallet on the east side walkway.

Even though District supervisors have consistently voted the barrier measure down, consultants and Bridge staff continued working on various designs assisted by the suicide prevention bureaus of San Francisco and Marin county. One model was extensively modified but various components were found not to perform as required. Proposal Number 16 was proven to be an effective suicide barrier but its appearance was "very cumbersome and not very attractive." This model now resides in the Bridge's "boneyard" near the Toll Plaza.

In 1993 the board declined to authorize proceeding with a final design and construction of a suicide barrier, but passed an article stating "any future district design activity for long-range bridge projects...shall include consideration of a suicide deterrent."

When a father threw his 3-year-old daughter over the railing in 1993, (See Chapter Six) there was another hew and cry for a barrier.

Eve Myer, executive director of the San Francisco Suicide Prevention Center, which, in 1962, was the first in the nation, said, "A tragedy like this recent one brings home the fact that as a community we need to sit down and say what are aesthetics worth to us, what is the money worth to us... Should we try to prevent--not all--but most of these...and should we all start taking more responsibility for each other."

Asked if suicide barriers would ever become a reality, she laughed quietly, fell silent for a bit, then said: "I have no idea. I have no idea. I would like to see barriers go up but I don't think they will. I don't know any circumstances under which they would. I honestly don't understand it all."

Myer believes the actual number of suicides from the Bridge is "probably twice as high as the official list." Although the suicide rate in San Francisco is well above the national average, Myer said "there are at least ten cities in the U.S. that have a higher suicide rate than we have, most of them in Florida and Nevada." She does not believe the argument that if people can't use the Bridge to end their lives, they will simply go elsewhere and cited the Seiden study which tracked would-be Bridge leapers for 20 years after their attempt and found that only 15 percent went on to take their lives.

Myer's counterpart in Marin County is Alan Johnson, Executive Director for the County's Suicide Prevention and Community Counseling Center, which has been in existence for 25 years.

"Our interest is suicide in general and the Bridge just collaterally," he said. "I can't say we've got a position with regard to suicide barriers, but the Board talks about it from time to time and I've written letters and attended meetings with the Bridge District people. We're not representing a lobby or anything like that. We're just concerned like we are with suicide at San Quentin or anywhere else. We're in dialogue with the Bridge people right now and we continue to meet. They are genuine about wanting to prevent suicides but they have some engineering problems. So we continue to try to find a solution. Solutions have been found at other sites, such as the Eiffel Tower, the Empire State Building and other bridges and I think a solution could be found here too. I think it's up to me and others to continue to work toward finding a solution. That's the approach I'm taking."

Although the border between San Francisco and Marin counties is at the center of the Bridge, Marin has chosen to let the emergency phones on the span be channeled to the San Francisco suicide prevention agency. However, even though people can now be patched into the agency's hot line, few have used this option.

"I don't know why that is," said Johnson, "maybe they've made up their minds by the time they reach the Bridge. People who are suicidal are ambivalent and if you can stop them or intervene...that's the business we're in. We contract with people sometimes for minutes, sometimes for hours on the phone. We've even had situations where we've heard the gun clicking and people told us they had the razor blade on their wrists and we know they've got pills or ingested the pills. We talk them into putting the gun away, setting the knife down, going to the hospital and having their stomach pumped, with the understanding that they call us in an hour, then in five hours and again in 24 hours. Those kinds of people frequently survive. We'll save lives if we can intervene in those threatened suicides. It's not as though if the Bridge were not available to them they're going to go some place else, because just in moving to another place they may change their minds. That's why we very much encourage a suicide

Donner

barrier. We think any other prevention method will be very small in relation to what a barrier would do."

Joyce Pavlovsky, heading a grassroots group known as Bridgewatch, has been fighting for a barrier down the center of the span to prevent "head-ons" as well as for a suicide barrier for more than 20 years. She called the Bridge "an attractive nuisance."

"Our Bridge is so beautiful and means so many things to many people, but it also has the reputation that people can throw themselves over for whatever reason and that's tragic," she said.

"Since 1972 I've been trying to make the Bridge safer for traffic, especially Doyle Drive (*the southern ramp leading to the Bridge notorious for accidents*). The reason I got involved with suicides is because you zero in on the Bridge for one thing and it automatically takes you into another. The husband of a friend of mine jumped off the Bridge and left her in a terrible state with three children. It just doesn't seem right to me with people jumping off left and right and Bridge officials not working harder to come up with a solution.

"In 1993 they came up with recommendations such as a more powerful camera on the north side where they can't see so well from the Bridge captain's office," Pavlovsky said. "So they are planning and pricing out a stronger camera that will pick up all activity on the north side of the Bridge. They're also discussing the possibility of hiring special guards to patrol during the times when most suicides occur. They have studies and graphs and pretty well know when most suicides take place. But the only real way to stop people from jumping is to close the Bridge to pedestrians, but of course that would take away all the tourist business and I'm

Donner

sure members of the District would not vote for that.

"Will there ever be a suicide barrier on the Bridge? No. At least not in my lifetime. It'll never come out of committee. I'll never see a barrier down the middle of the roadway either.

"A lot of people say they don't want anybody to touch the Bridge in anyway because it will spoil the look. It is a national treasure and people love it the way it is. Nobody's going to come up with a design that will be pleasing to everyone. There are some new people on the Board who are very supportive of the recent recommendations about the cameras and special guards. But you will not get a suicide barrier. They've stopped listening," said Pavlovsky.

A Bridge district engineer responded that the board "was sensitive to the feelings of the public" and would probably look at the issue again if prompted by public opinion.

In 1995 the District announced a $170 million seismic and strengthening retrofit and had already earmarked $30 million for the project. The challenge facing the District at this time was to secure federal funds for the five-year project. It cost $13.3 million for the retrofit design that would allow the Bridge to withstand an 8.3 quake and winds up to 100 mph. Engineers said the Loma Prieta quake in 1989, which was measured at 7.1, had stressed the Bridge to its maximum. The Bridge cost $35 million to build in 1937, but its replacement cost today is estimated at $1.4 billion.

After considerable debate, no plan for a suicide barrier was included in this huge project. The District Board stated a suicide barrier was not included because it "would require an historical value study and have the potential effect of delaying or stopping the deck replacement project and/or jeopardizing the limited federal funding that was available

Donner

for that project."

There have been other suggestions to curtail jumps from the Bridge, such as: a) limit pedestrian and cyclist use, b) totally prohibit all pedestrian and cyclist use, and c) allow people on the Bridge only with a guided tour.

The obvious shortcomings of these suggestions, however, are that a person would still be able to drive onto the span, stop and jump. As for guided tours, it's not difficult to imagine someone in a tour group suddenly mount the railing and plunge spectacularly into the next world, watched by a stunned tour group.

Made in the USA
San Bernardino, CA
14 May 2017